JIM FOBEL'S
DIET FEASTS

OTHER BOOKS BY JIM FOBEL

*JIM FOBEL'S OLD-FASHIONED BAKING BOOK
*BEAUTIFUL FOOD
*THE BIG BOOK OF FABULOUS FUN-FILLED CELEBRATIONS
AND HOLIDAY CRAFTS (co-author)
*THE STENCIL BOOK (co-author)

JIM FOBEL'S
DIET FEASTS
AN INSPIRED NEW CUISINE

Healthy, Hearty, Delicious

Jim Fobel

Produced by Jane Ross Associates, Inc.
and Bellwether Books

DOUBLEDAY
NEW YORK LONDON TORONTO SYDNEY AUCKLAND

Acknowledgments
Special thanks to: Brown Cranna, John Duff, Dennis Galante,
Lynn Hill, David Michael Kennedy, Judith Kern, Hiroko Kiiffner,
Jane Littell, Mardee Haidin Regan, Bill Rose, Jane Ross,
Tom Russell, Jerry Simpson, and Liz Trovato.

Published by Doubleday, a division of Bantam Doubleday Dell
Publishing Group, Inc., 666 Fifth Avenue, New York, NY 10103

Doubleday and the portrayal of an anchor with a dolphin are
trademarks of Doubleday, a division of the Bantam Doubleday
Dell Publishing Group, Inc.

Library of Congress Cataloging-in-Publication Data
Fobel, Jim.
[Diet feasts]
Jim Fobel's diet feasts / by Jim Fobel.—1st ed.
p. cm.
"Produced by Jane Ross Associates, Inc., and Bellwether Books."
Includes index.
ISBN 0–385–26001–6
1. Low-calorie diet—Recipes. I. Title. II. Title: Diet feasts.
RM222.2.F63 1989   89-35091
641.5′635—dc20   CIP

Certain of these recipes were previously published in
Food & Wine, Bon Appetit and *Chocolatier* magazines.

Photographs of *Red and Green Roasted Pepper Lasagne,
Vegetarian Chili, Sautéed Codfish Cakes, Broiled Marinated
Chicken with Vegetables,* and *Zesty Lemon Cake Roll* copyright
©1990 by Jerry Simpson; *Calico Shepherd's Pie* and *Stir-Fried
Shrimp and Chinese Vegetables* copyright ©1987 by David
Michael Kennedy; *Cheese Enchiladas* copyright ©1987
by Dennis Galante.

Designed by Liz Trovato

For my ever-lovin' Auntie Myra

CONTENTS

INTRODUCTION

I love food. And since I am a big person, I'm always looking for generous portions of *real* food, made from the best ingredients with truly robust flavor. Then I'm happy.

Dieting, however, makes me unhappy. Whether it's a weight-loss regimen or meant solely to promote better health, diets have never really worked for me — they're too restrictive. Eating tasteless little dishes of boring food inevitably leaves me feeling deprived, frustrated and, most of all, *hungry*.

Convinced that I, as a health-conscious food lover, could do better, I set myself the task of creating great-tasting recipes that suit my moods and appetite, while still satisfying my nutritional needs. My goal was to devise recipes for large portions of delicious, comforting food that would be good for me.

I think I did it. I "conquered" all of the favorite dishes that I'd normally have to give up on a health and weight-loss diet: pizza, stuffed pasta shells, linguine with white clam sauce and lasagne (in several varieties); tacos, enchiladas and moussaka; New England clam chowder, Coquilles St. Jacques and crispy fried sole; bleu cheese dressing and old-fashioned potato salad. I discovered that I could control the calorie count as well as the fat, protein, carbohydrate, sodium and cholesterol content in these recipes without sacrificing the flavor or essential character of the dish. The result is that each recipe in this book contains fewer than 350 calories per serving, and many have considerably fewer.

Here are recipes for every type of menu or occasion — a casual weekday lunch or weekend brunch, hors d'oeuvres for a cocktail party or a formal dinner, dishes ideal for picnics, intimate suppers and lavish buffets. There are snacks and side dishes, soups and stews. Some of the salads and vegetable dishes — such as the fresh tuna salad with roasted peppers or zucchini parmigiana — make wonderful main-course entrées. You really can indulge yourself, take a look at the pasta, pie and pancake chapter, without straying from the guidelines of good nutrition.

These days, I practically live on my low-calorie versions of shepherd's pie or meat loaf along with mashed potatoes and gravy, and proudly serve seafood sukiyaki, chicken jambalaya or Chinese flash-fried lamb to my guests. And if you crave dessert after dinner, you'll love my Spanish-style chocolate flan, peach melba terrine with raspberry sauce, zesty lemon cake roll, strawberry champagne zabaglione or apple crisp.

These hearty diet dishes are for feasting and for fun — for people who care about food as much as I do.

Jim Fobel
New York City

AUTHOR'S NOTE

The nutritional analysis of each recipe is based on a single serving unless otherwise noted.

These recipes contain minimal amounts of fat and cholesterol. According to current nutritional guidelines, consumption of fat should be no more than 30% of one's total calorie intake *per day* (*not per meal*); cholesterol less than 250 to 300 milligrams daily.

In certain recipes, however, I have chosen to use limited quantities of whole milk for its richness and flavor. If you need to further reduce the number of calories in your diet, substitute low-fat or skim milk for the whole milk, but expect a somewhat blander result.

With regard to sodium, most recipes call for a specific quantity of salt, well within the recommended daily maximum of 2,000 to 3,000 milligrams (1/2 teaspoon of salt contains 1,100 milligrams of sodium). In some instances, the recipe calls for salt to taste; add small amounts, starting with a pinch.

CHAPTER ONE

GREAT BEGINNINGS

Think small, light and delicious in considering these alternatives to standard cocktail-party fare. Intensely flavored fresh tomato canapés, broccoli "mops" in ginger sauce, stuffed mushrooms and stuffed clams, more adventurous homemade shrimp sausages or chicken and scallion dumplings: All make great hors d'oeuvres or appetizers or combine into appealing antipasto selections.

BROCCOLI MOPS WITH GINGER SAUCE *Little*
"mops" of broccoli (upside-down broccoli florets) sop up a platterful of luscious ginger sauce. They make a great hot hors d'œuvre or vegetable side dish.

MAKES 8 HORS D'OEUVRE SERVINGS OR 4 VEGETABLE SERVINGS

1 large head of broccoli cut into 40 small florets (1 pound)
1 tablespoon cornstarch
1 cup canned beef broth or stock
1 tablespoon dry sherry
1 tablespoon soy sauce
2 teaspoons rice vinegar
1 teaspoon sugar
1 teaspoon vegetable oil
1 tablespoon minced fresh ginger
1 medium garlic clove, minced or crushed through a press
1 teaspoon Oriental sesame oil
3 medium scallions, thinly sliced

1. Bring a large pot of lightly salted water to a boil over high heat. Drop in the broccoli and cook just until tender, about 3 minutes after the water returns to a boil. Drain. Cover with aluminum foil to keep hot.

2. In a small bowl, stir together the cornstarch, stock, sherry, soy sauce, vinegar and sugar. In a small heavy saucepan, combine the vegetable oil, ginger and garlic. Sizzle over moderate heat for about 1 minute. Give the sauce mixture a good stir to blend the cornstarch; add it to the pan. Stirring constantly, cook the ginger sauce over moderate heat until thickened and boiling. Stir in the sesame oil and scallions and remove from the heat.

3. Pour the sauce onto a warmed serving platter. Arrange the broccoli florets upside down in the gravy (stems up). Serve hot.

NOTE: Nutritional values given below refer to a single hors d'oeuvre serving.

Calories *39*   **Protein** *3 gm*   **Fat** *2 gm*   **Carbohydrate** *6 gm*   **Sodium** *245 mg*   **Cholesterol** *0 mg*

THREE-TOMATO CANAPÉS *The intense sweet flavor of Italian sun-dried tomatoes complements fresh tomatoes and tomato paste in these triple-flavored treats. They should be made no more than an hour or two ahead.*

MAKES 2 DOZEN

1 small (3-ounce) package cream cheese, at room temperature
2 tablespoons tomato paste
12 thin slices whole wheat bread
4 small Italian plum tomatoes, sliced ¼ inch thick
Salt and coarsely cracked black pepper
1 ounce (8 halves) Italian sun-dried tomatoes in olive oil, well-drained on paper towels

1. Put the cream cheese into a medium bowl and mash in the tomato paste with a fork until evenly blended.
2. Using a 2-inch round cutter, cut 24 rounds from the whole wheat bread. Spread each with 1 teaspoon of the tomato-cheese mixture. Top each with a tomato slice; sprinkle lightly with salt and generously with pepper. Cut the sun-dried tomatoes into ¹⁄₁₆-inch slivers. Sprinkle over the canapés and serve, or cover and chill for a brief time.
NOTE: Nutritional values given below refer to a single canapé.

Calories 30 *Protein 1 gm* *Fat 2 gm* *Carbohydrate 3 gm* *Sodium 74 mg* *Cholesterol 4 mg*

MUSHROOM-STUFFED MUSHROOMS *Delicious and moist, these stuffed mushroom caps make a first-rate hors d'oeuvre or antipasto.*

MAKES 18

18 medium mushrooms (1 pound)
1 small (2-ounce) onion, grated
1/3 cup freshly grated Parmesan cheese
1/4 cup plain dry bread crumbs
1/2 teaspoon dried basil, crumbled
1/4 teaspoon dried oregano, crumbled
Pinch of salt
3 tablespoons dry white wine
1 tablespoon milk
1 tablespoon olive oil
Lemon wedges (optional)

1. Adjust a shelf to the top third of the oven and preheat to 375°. Have ready a 12-by-8-inch baking pan.

2. Break off the stems from the mushrooms so each cap is left with a hollow cavity for stuffing. Finely chop or coarsely grate the stems into a medium bowl. Add the onion and all but 1 tablespoon of the Parmesan. Stir in the bread crumbs, basil, oregano, salt, 1 tablespoon of the wine and all of the milk to make a slightly dry stuffing.

3. Arrange the mushroom caps upside down (hollow cavity up) in the baking dish. Lightly brush the rims with the oil. Stuff each cap, using about 1 tablespoon for each, mounding, but not packing, the filling. Sprinkle the tops with the reserved 1 tablespoon Parmesan. Add the remaining 2 tablespoons wine along with 2 tablespoons water to the pan, around the mushrooms. Bake until golden brown on top, 15 to 17 minutes. Serve hot, with lemon wedges, if desired.

NOTE: Nutritional values given below refer to a single stuffed mushroom.

Calories 27	*Protein* 1 gm	*Fat* 1 gm	*Carbohydrate* 3 gm	*Sodium* 46 mg	*Cholesterol* 1 mg

CAPONATA

This classic eggplant antipasto of Italy, a relative of the French ratatouille, is usually made with buckets of olive oil. My version requires just 1 tablespoon because the eggplants are broiled rather than sautéed. As an appetizer this caponata enhances most pasta dishes or the Stuffed Polenta (page 169) and I love it alongside My Skinny Cheeseburgers (page 170). Serve it chilled or at room temperature.

MAKES 16 SERVINGS OF ½ CUP EACH

- 2 large (1½ pounds each) firm, slender eggplants (they should feel heavy for their size)
- 1 tablespoon olive oil
- 3 medium (4-ounce) onions, cut lengthwise into ¼-inch-wide slivers
- 2 cups diced (½-inch) celery (preferably heart or tender inner stalks)
- 1 large garlic clove, minced or crushed through a press
- 1 can (28-ounce) whole tomatoes
- ⅓ cup red wine vinegar
- 2 tablespoons sugar
- 1 teaspoon dried basil, crumbled
- 1 teaspoon dried oregano, crumbled
- ¼ teaspoon black pepper
- ½ cup sliced pimiento-stuffed green olives
- ½ cup sliced pitted black ripe olives
- Salt

1. Preheat the broiler. Prick the eggplants all over with a long fork. Place on a double layer of aluminum foil. Broil until charred on one side and soft within, 10 to 12 minutes. Turn and broil for 10 to 12 minutes longer until charred and the eggplant is soft throughout. Remove, drain off all liquid and let stand on the foil until cool enough to handle. Preheat the oven to 350°. Carefully peel off just the skin; coarsely chop the eggplants.

2. Spoon the olive oil into a nonreactive large skillet and place over moderate heat. Add the onions and celery; sauté, stirring frequently, until softened and lightly colored (adding 1 or 2 tablespoons of water whenever the vegetables seem dry), about 5 minutes. Add the garlic and cook for 1 minute longer. Drain the tomatoes in a strainer over a bowl; cut them in quarters. Add the tomato pieces and ½ cup of the juice to the pan. Stir in the vinegar, sugar, basil, oregano and pepper. Bring to a boil and cook over moderately high heat for 5 minutes to evaporate some of the liquid. Add the chopped eggplant and toss.

3. Turn the caponata into a large baking

dish. Bake, uncovered, for 30 minutes. Remove from the oven and stir in the green and black olives and salt to taste.

Let cool to room temperature; cover and chill. Serve cold, cool or at room temperature.

Calories 69   **Protein** 2 gm   **Fat** 3 gm   **Carbohydrate** 12 gm   **Sodium** 232 mg   **Cholesterol** 0 mg

---

CHINESE CHICKEN DUMPLINGS WITH ORANGE DIPPING SAUCE

This excellent recipe makes use of packaged wonton wrappers (available in Oriental markets) and a technique used to make the classic "pot stickers" (crusty fried dumplings). The filling, however, is made from lean chicken, spinach and cabbage, instead of fatty pork.

MAKES 4 DOZEN

3/4 pound skinless boned chicken thighs
2 tablespoons vegetable oil
1 1/2 cups finely chopped green cabbage
1 cup cooked, chopped, well-drained
   spinach
1 large whole egg
1 tablespoon minced fresh ginger
3 medium scallions, finely minced
   (about 1/4 cup)
1 tablespoon reduced-sodium soy sauce
1 small garlic clove, minced or crushed
   through a press
Pinch of salt
1 egg yolk
48 medium-thick store-bought wonton
   skins (about 9 ounces)

ORANGE DIPPING SAUCE:

1/3 cup strained fresh orange juice
1/3 cup canned chicken broth or stock
   (page 31)
1 tablespoon reduced-sodium soy sauce
1 teaspoon Oriental sesame oil
1 teaspoon rice vinegar
1 scallion, finely minced

1. Cut the chicken into 1-inch cubes. Grind to a fine texture with a food processor or meat grinder.

2. Spoon 2 teaspoons of the vegetable oil into a large heavy skillet and place over moderate heat. Add the cabbage and sauté until soft and translucent and beginning to scorch. Add 1 to 2 tablespoons of water anytime the cabbage begins to dry out or stick and continue cooking until medium golden brown, 4 to 5 minutes. Set aside to cool to room temperature.

3. Put the ground chicken in a large bowl and stir in the cabbage and spinach. Add the whole egg, ginger, scallions, soy sauce, garlic and salt. Mix with your hands in a circular motion until well blended.

4. In a cup, whisk the egg yolk and 2 teaspoons water. Keep the wonton skins covered while working or they will dry out. One at a time, place a wonton skin in front of you and spoon 1 tablespoon of the filling in the center. Dip a butter knife or your fingertip into the diluted egg yolk and brush two of the edges. Fold the wonton skin up over the filling to make a triangle so the top two points are slightly askew and pinch to enclose, squeezing out any air as you do so. Dab a little egg yolk on the right side point and bring left and right side points together, overlapping them by about ½-inch. Pinch together (the wonton will resemble a nurse's cap). Repeat, shaping all of the wontons.

5. PREPARE THE ORANGE DIPPING SAUCE: In a small bowl, stir together the orange juice, broth, soy sauce, sesame oil, vinegar and scallion. Serve in tiny shallow bowls for dipping the wontons.

6. You will need to work in two batches, or use two 10-inch skillets to cook the dumplings. In a heavy well-seasoned skillet, heat 2 teaspoons of the remaining oil over moderate heat. Add half of the wontons, points upward, and cook until deep golden brown on the bottom, 2 to 3 minutes. Add ½ cup water. Cover and steam until the water evaporates, 2 to 3 minutes longer. Uncover and cook for 1 to 2 minutes to make the bottoms crispy. Repeat with the remaining wontons and oil.

7. Serve hot with dipping sauce.

NOTE: Nutritional values given below refer to a single dumpling.

Calories 38   *Protein* 2 gm   *Fat* 1 gm   *Carbohydrate* 4 gm   *Sodium* 46 mg   *Cholesterol* 17 mg

---

CEVICHE del JARDIN
In Mexico, I learned this trick of combining lime juice with fresh coconut juice to impart a delicate flavor to ceviche. However, if you cannot find a good fresh coconut, simply omit it. Serve it as a salad course on lettuce leaves or as an hors d'oeuvre, filling endive spears.

MAKES 8 SALAD SERVINGS OF ½ CUP EACH

1½ pounds very fresh fish fillets, such as cod, halibut, mackerel or sole, or scallops, or half and half of two varieties, cut into ½-inch cubes

1 cup fresh lime juice (from about 8 medium limes)

¾ cup strained fresh coconut juice (see NOTE)

½ cup sliced pimiento-stuffed green olives

2 tablespoons olive oil

1 jalapeño chile pepper (or more to taste), seeded and minced

¼ teaspoon dried oregano, crumbled

¼ teaspoon ground cumin

2 medium-large (4-ounce) plum tomatoes, cut into ½-inch dice

¼ cup thinly sliced scallions

2 tablespoons chopped cilantro (fresh coriander)

Salt and pepper

8 medium romaine lettuce leaves, or 60 Belgian endive leaves

1 medium firm-ripe California avocado, cut into 8 wedges and peeled (optional)

NOTE: Choose a medium-size (relatively heavy) fresh coconut that contains plenty of liquid (shake it). Pierce the three eyes with nail and hammer and let drain over a glass; strain. If the water smells sour or tastes fermented, discard it.

1. Put the fish into a medium nonreactive bowl with the lime juice and coconut water. Cover and chill for 12 hours or overnight, stirring once in a while. Drain, reserving ½ cup of the marinade.

2. Return the marinated fish to the bowl. It will now appear to be cooked, that is, opaque throughout. Add the olives, olive oil, jalapeño, oregano, cumin and ¼ cup of the reserved marinade. Stir in the diced tomatoes, scallions and cilantro. Season with salt and pepper to taste. Cover and chill for an hour or longer. (**The recipe can be prepared a day ahead to this point.**) Let come to room temperature for 30 minutes, just to take away the icy chill.

3. To assemble, place a lettuce leaf on each of 8 salad plates. Top each with about ½ cup of ceviche. Dip the avocado wedges into the remaining ¼ cup reserved marinade and place 1 wedge on each salad. Serve cold. To serve as an hors d'œuvre, spoon 1 tablespoon on each endive spear.

Calories 131   *Protein* 16 gm   *Fat* 5 gm   *Carbohydrate* 6 gm   *Sodium* 277 mg   *Cholesterol* 37 mg

SHRIMP SAUSAGES

S HRIMP SAUSAGES *Here is a deliciously different use for fresh shrimp. You will need a meat grinder and a sausage stuffer to make them (but in a pinch a processor and a funnel will do). You will also need hog casing for sausage-making (available at some butcher shops). Serve the sausages hot or cold with Cocktail Sauce and/or Creamy "Mayonnaise" Dressing (pages 20 and 54).*

MAKES 18

1 pound medium-large raw shrimp, shelled, deveined and tails removed
1 pound skinless sole or cod fillets, cut into 1-by-2-inch strips
4 medium fresh jalapeño chile peppers (see NOTE)
1/3 cup lightly packed chopped cilantro (fresh coriander)
4 large egg whites
2 tablespoons fresh lemon juice
1 teaspoon ground cumin
1 1/2 teaspoons salt
1/4 teaspoon black pepper
6 feet of hog casing for sausages, in a continuous length

NOTE: The heat of chile peppers is contained in its seeds and ribs. Their volatile oils are harsh irritants so it is safest to wear rubber gloves when handling them (though I never bother with this myself). Quarter the chiles lengthwise, then cut off the ribs and seeds and discard them. (If you want the sausages to be hot, leave some of them in.) You should have about 1/4 cup minced jalapeños.

1. Put the shrimp and sole through the coarse blade of a meat grinder. In a large bowl, combine the ground seafood with the jalapeños, cilantro, egg whites, lemon juice, cumin, salt and pepper. Mix well with your hands or a large spoon.

2. Rinse the hog casing in cold water and then let cold water run through it directly from the tap. Thread the casing onto a sausage stuffer (on the meat grinder). Tie a knot at one end.

3. Put the seafood mixture back through the grinder and let it grind through, into the casing. As you hold the filled casing, let 2-inches remain unfilled near the knot to allow room for expansion. Do not overstuff the casing. The sausage should be about 1-inch wide and can be squeezed gently to make it an even width. You will have about 5 feet of sausage. Tie a knot at the other end, again leaving 2 inches of casing to allow for expansion during cooking.

4. Pour 1 inch of water into a large heavy skillet; bring to a boil over high heat. Reduce the heat so that the water barely simmers. Carefully coil the sausage into the water and prick it at 3-inch intervals with a toothpick. Cover the pan and poach gently for 10 minutes. Remove from the heat; let stand 10 minutes longer. If serving cold, let cool to room temperature before chilling. To serve hot, simply cut into 3-inch lengths (or thin slices to make an hors d'oeuvre). Serve hot or cold.

NOTE: Nutritional values given below refer to a single sausage.

Calories 50	*Protein* 10 gm	*Fat* 1 gm	*Carbohydrate* 1 gm	*Sodium* 246 mg	*Cholesterol* 43 mg

COCKTAIL SAUCE *Serve this nippy sauce with the Shrimp Sausages on page 19.*

MAKES ¾ CUP OR 12 SERVINGS OF 1 TABLESPOON EACH

⅔ cup Heinz chili sauce
1 tablespoon drained prepared white horseradish
1 tablespoon fresh lemon juice
2 to 3 drops Tabasco sauce or other hot pepper sauce

1. Combine the chili sauce and horseradish in a small bowl. Stir in the lemon juice and Tabasco sauce. Serve cold.

Calories 16	*Protein* 0 gm	*Fat* 0 gm	*Carbohydrate* 4 gm	*Sodium* 171 mg	*Cholesterol* 0 mg

HOT MUSSEL ANTIPASTO *Here is a great hot antipasto or first course before dinner. I make a meal of them for lunch sometimes. They are economical, delicious, low in calories, and guaranteed to start your mouth watering for the pasta course to come.*

MAKES 6 SERVINGS

5 pounds fresh live mussels
1 cup dry white wine
½ cup finely diced carrot
½ cup finely diced celery
⅓ cup chopped parsley
1 large garlic clove, sliced
1 bay leaf
⅛ teaspoon dried red hot pepper flakes
4 medium scallions, thinly sliced
6 lemon slices

1. Put the mussels into a large bowl or sinkful of cool water. Yank the seaweed beard from each and scrub the mussels. Rinse and drain.

2. In a large nonreactive pot, combine the wine, carrot, celery, parsley, garlic, bay leaf and hot pepper flakes. Bring to a boil over moderately high heat. Reduce the heat to low and simmer for 3 minutes.

3. Add the mussels, cover the pot, and turn the heat to high. Cook until the mussels open, stirring or tossing once or twice, 3 to 5 minutes. Discard any that do not open or that cannot be pried open easily. Remove from the heat and stir in the scallions. Divide among 6 shallow soup bowls and top each with a lemon slice. Serve hot.

Calories *110* **Protein** *14 gm* **Fat** *3 gm* **Carbohydrate** *9 gm* **Sodium** *330 mg* **Cholesterol** *31 mg*

COLD MUSSELS WITH TWO SAUCES *A tray of these festive-looking mussels makes an attractive party hors d'oeuvre or antipasto, or even a light luncheon entrée.*

MAKES 5 DOZEN

5 dozen (5 pounds) medium mussels
½ cup dry white wine
2 medium garlic cloves, minced or
    crushed through a press

GREEN SAUCE:
¼ cup heavy cream
1 bunch watercress, largest stems
    removed (2 cups)
1 cup chopped parsley
2 tablespoons mayonnaise
¼ teaspoon black pepper

SOUR CREAM-DILL SAUCE:
⅓ cup sour cream
¼ cup plain lowfat yogurt
2 tablespoons mayonnaise
3 tablespoons snipped fresh dill
1 tablespoon fresh lemon juice

1. PREPARE THE MUSSELS: Put the mussels into a large bowl or sinkful of cold water. Yank out the seaweed beards that protrude near the hinge. Scrub the mussels with a brush; rinse. In a large nonreactive pot, combine the mussels, wine and garlic. Cover and cook over high heat until they open, 3 to 5 minutes. Discard any mussels that do not open. Remove and set aside until cool enough to handle. Reserve 1 cup of the cooking liquid for the green sauce; discard the rest.

2. With a small spoon or your fingers, scoop the mussels from their shells and drain them on paper towels. Twist the shells to separate them at the hinge. Reserve 5 dozen half-shells. Rinse and drain them; pat dry with paper towels. Arrange them on one or two platters that will fit in the refrigerator. Place one mussel in each half shell and chill for at least 30 minutes. If chilling longer, cover with plastic.

3. PREPARE THE GREEN SAUCE: Pour the reserved 1 cup mussel cooking liquid into a small nonreactive saucepan. Boil over moderately high heat until reduced to ⅓ cup, about 5 minutes. Add the cream and boil until reduced to ⅓ cup, 3 to 5 minutes. Let cool to room temperature.

4. Bring a medium pot of water to a boil over high heat. Drop in the watercress and parsley and cook for exactly 1 minute from the time they hit the water. Drain well. Set aside to cool to room temperature. Squeeze out any excess water.
5. In a food processor or blender, combine the greens and the reduced mussel/cream mixture with the mayonnaise and black pepper. Process to a purée. If making ahead, cover and chill.

6. **PREPARE THE SOUR CREAM-DILL SAUCE:** In a small bowl, whisk together the sour cream, yogurt and mayonnaise. Whisk in the dill and lemon juice. If making ahead, cover and chill.
7. Spoon about 1 teaspoon of the green sauce over 30 of the mussels and about 1 teaspoon of the sour cream-dill sauce over the rest. If not serving right away, chill. Serve cold.
NOTE: Nutritional values given below refer to a single prepared mussel.

| Calories 24 | Protein 1 gm | Fat 2 gm | Carbohydrate 1 gm | Sodium 43 mg | Cholesterol 6 mg |

STUFFED CLAMS OREGANATA *You will need fresh cherrystone clams to make this addictive antipasto or appetizer (but I confess to making a meal of them on occasion.) An English muffin, ground in a food processor and toasted, makes great fresh bread crumbs and is a good way to control the calorie count. Since these clams are large, only a dozen is needed to make 16 stuffed clams!*

MAKES 16

1 dozen large (3-inch) cherrystone clams
1 English muffin (2 ounces)
1 tablespoon olive oil
1 medium (4-ounce) onion, finely chopped
¾ cup finely chopped celery
1 medium garlic clove, minced or crushed through a press
¼ cup finely chopped parsley, preferably flat-leaf Italian
¼ cup freshly grated Parmesan cheese (1 ounce)
½ teaspoon dried oregano, crumbled
⅛ teaspoon black pepper
Pinch of salt
Lemon wedges

1. Put the clams in a large bowl of cold water and scrub them with a brush. Rinse well. Transfer the clams to a large heavy pot, cover, and place over high heat. Steam until the clams open, 4 to 5 minutes. Remove with tongs and let drain upside down in a colander set over a bowl. When cool enough to handle, twist the shells to separate the halves and scoop out the clams with a small spoon. Reserve ¼ cup of the clam juice for the stuffing and discard the rest (you will have ¾ to 1 cup and you could reserve it for another use, if you have one, but the clam juice can be very salty). If any of the clams have not opened but can be easily pried open with a knife or spoon, they probably are fine; if they resist prying, discard them.) Wash and dry 16 of the half-shells and discard the rest.

2. Preheat the oven to 400°. Grind the English muffin into coarse bread crumbs in a food processor (or tear into small pieces and then crumble further after toasting). Place the crumbs on a sheet of aluminum foil or on a small baking sheet and toast until golden brown and dry, 5 to 8 minutes. Remove from the oven and increase the heat to **broil.**

3. Spoon the olive oil into a heavy medium skillet and place over moderate heat. Add the onion and celery and sauté until softened, 3 to 5 minutes. Add the garlic and cook 30 seconds longer. Remove from the heat and stir in the toasted bread crumbs, parsley, half of the Parmesan, the oregano, pepper and salt. Stir in the reserved ¼ cup clam juice.

4. Cut each clam into 6 or 8 pieces. Line a large broiler pan with aluminum foil and arrange the 16 half-shells on it. Divide the clams among the shells (about 1 tablespoon per shell) and top with the crumb mixture (using one generous tablespoonful for each, and dividing it equally). Sprinkle the remaining Parmesan over the tops. Broil until golden brown and a light crust forms over the tops, 3 to 6 minutes. Serve hot, with lemon wedges.

NOTE: Nutritional values given below refer to a single stuffed clam.

Calories 38   *Protein* 3 gm   *Fat* 2 gm   *Carbohydrate* 3 gm   *Sodium* 69 mg   *Cholesterol* 6 mg

---

LITTLE SOUPS & BIG SOUPS

A little soup—a fragrant fresh tomato with cilantro, perhaps—may awaken your taste buds yet curb your appetite before lunch or dinner. Creamy mushroom or corn tortilla soups make for perfect summer luncheons on the terrace. And a big soup— minestrone or one of the chowders or chiles—makes a hearty, subtle and satisfying meal unto itself.

FRESH TOMATO-CILANTRO SOUP *This deliciously fragrant soup relies on the flavor of fresh tomatoes and cilantro (fresh coriander) and is best prepared with homemade chicken stock (recipe, page 31). If you can't obtain fresh cilantro use fresh basil or ⅛ teaspoon saffron. Although not figured in the calorie count, a tablespoon of sour cream (30 calories) can be spooned onto each serving, as a garnish, along with a few toasted croutons.*

*MAKES 6 SERVINGS OF
1 CUP EACH*

2 pounds fresh tomatoes
1 tablespoon olive oil
2 medium (4-ounce) onions, chopped
*1 medium (2-ounce) carrot, peeled and
    coarsely shredded or chopped*
*1 large garlic clove, minced or crushed
    through a press*
*1 quart chicken stock (page 31) or
    canned broth*
⅓ cup long-grain white rice
½ bay leaf
¼ teaspoon dried basil, crumbled
¼ teaspoon dried thyme, crumbled
1 teaspoon salt
⅛ teaspoon black pepper
1 teaspoon sugar (optional)
*3 tablespoons finely chopped cilantro
    (fresh coriander)*

1. Peel the tomatoes either by skewering one at a time onto a long fork and turning slowly over a gas flame until blistered all over or by dropping into boiling water for 10 seconds and then dipping into cold water. In either case, the skin can then be pulled or rubbed off. Halve the tomatoes crosswise and then gently squeeze out the seeds. Cut out and discard the stem end and chop the tomatoes; you will have 2½ to 3 cups chopped.

2. Spoon the oil into a nonreactive medium saucepan or soup pot. Over moderate heat, add the onions and carrot and sauté until softened, about 5 minutes. Add the garlic and cook for 1 minute longer. Add the tomatoes, chicken stock, rice, bay leaf, basil, thyme and salt. Bring to a boil, stirring frequently, over moderate heat. Reduce the heat, partially cover, and simmer, stirring once in awhile, until the rice is very tender, about 30 minutes. Remove from the heat; discard the bay leaf. Set aside to cool slightly. Purée the soup in a food processor or blender. Add the pepper, sugar and cilantro. Serve hot.

Calories 128   **Protein** *3 gm*   *Fat* *4 gm*   **Carbohydrate** *22 gm*   **Sodium** *385 mg*   **Cholesterol** *0 mg*

POTATO SOUP WITH SPRING GREENS *I love this simple hearty soup with its fresh greens. It is best when prepared with homemade chicken stock, and made several hours, or even a day, before you want to serve it.*

MAKES 8 SERVINGS OF
1 CUP EACH

4 to 6 medium leeks
2 teaspoons olive oil or other
  vegetable oil
¼ cup all-purpose flour
4 cups chicken stock (page 31) or
  canned broth
1½ cups milk
2 large (8-ounce) baking potatoes, peeled
  and cut into ½-inch dice
½ teaspoon dried basil, crumbled
½ bay leaf
⅛ teaspoon dried thyme, crumbled
1 teaspoon salt
¼ cup finely chopped parsley
2 medium scallions (including green
  stems), minced
2 tablespoons snipped chives (optional)
Black pepper

1. Trim off the darkest green portion of the leek stems and discard, leaving just the light and medium green parts. Cut the leeks in half lengthwise and then crosswise into ¼-inch slices. You will need 4 cups. Put the leeks in a large bowl of cold water and rinse well to remove any sand. Drain; roll up in several layers of paper towels to dry.

2. Spoon the oil into a large heavy saucepan or soup pot over moderate heat. Add the leeks and sauté until softened, adding 1 or 2 tablespoons of water if they begin to stick or become dry. Sprinkle with the flour and stir to moisten. Add the chicken stock and, stirring constantly, bring to a boil. Simmer for 1 minute. Add the milk, potatoes, basil, bay leaf, thyme and salt. Bring to a boil, stirring frequently. Reduce the heat, partially cover, and simmer, stirring occasionally, until the potatoes are very tender, 15 to 20 minutes.

3. Remove the soup from the heat; stir in the parsley and scallions. Ladle into hot soup plates. Sprinkle with the chives and a pinch of black pepper. Serve hot.

Calories 141   *Protein* 4 gm   *Fat* 4 gm   *Carbohydrate* 23 gm   *Sodium* 313 mg   *Cholesterol* 6 mg

---

CREAMY BROCCOLI SOUP *Robust and creamy-green, this tasty soup will surely satisfy any hungry person on a chilly day. It is best made with homemade chicken stock, but canned broth will do in a pinch.*

MAKES 6 SERVINGS OF
1 CUP EACH

1 pound of broccoli florets and stems, cut up (6 cups)
2 teaspoons olive oil
1 medium (4-ounce) onion, chopped
1 small garlic clove, minced or crushed through a press
¼ cup all-purpose flour
3 cups chicken stock (page 31) or canned broth
⅛ teaspoon dried basil, crumbled
⅛ teaspoon dried oregano, crumbled
⅛ teaspoon dried tarragon, crumbled
⅛ teaspoon dried thyme, crumbled
1 cup milk
1 to 2 tablespoons fresh lemon juice
¾ teaspoon salt

1. Bring a large pot of lightly salted water to a boil. Choose 6 perfect florets and drop them into the boiling water. Blanch for 1 to 2 minutes, until barely tender and still bright green. Remove with a slotted spoon and place in cold water; reserve for the garnish. Drop all of the rest of the broccoli into the boiling water and cook until very tender, about 7 minutes. Drain and let cool slightly.

2. In a heavy medium saucepan or soup pot, combine the oil and onion. Sauté over moderate heat until softened, 3 to 5 minutes. Add the garlic and cook for 15 seconds longer. Sprinkle on the flour and stir to blend. Pour in 2 cups of the chicken stock. Stir in the basil, oregano, tarragon and thyme. Stirring constantly, bring to a boil over moderate heat. Cook for 1 to 2 minutes until thickened. Allow to cool slightly. Combine in a blender or food processor with the broccoli and process to a purée.

3. Turn the purée into the pan. Add the milk and the remaining 1 cup stock. Bring to a boil, stirring. Reduce the heat and cook, stirring frequently, for 3 or 4 minutes. Stir in the lemon juice; season with salt. Ladle into soup plates; garnish each portion with a reserved broccoli floret. Serve hot.

Calories 107   *Protein* 5 gm   *Fat* 4 gm   *Carbohydrate* 14 gm   *Sodium* 317 mg   *Cholesterol* 6 mg

CORN TORTILLA SOUP *So good and hearty, this soup makes me day-dream about past trips to Mexico as soon as I start preparing it. It will be best if you begin with homemade chicken stock (page 31), but canned or frozen will suffice.*

MAKES 8 SERVINGS OF
1 CUP EACH

1 tablespoon corn oil or other vegetable oil
2 medium (4-ounce) onions, chopped
2 large garlic cloves, minced or crushed
  through a press
4 medium (4-ounce) tomatoes, cored and
  roughly chopped
1 tablespoon ground cumin
1 tablespoon chili powder
1 bay leaf
¼ teaspoon dried oregano, crumbled
6 corn tortillas (6-inches in diameter)
¼ cup canned tomato sauce
2 teaspoons sugar
2 quarts chicken stock (page 31) or
  canned broth
1 medium skinless boned chicken breast
  half (6-ounces)
1 cup fresh, frozen or canned corn kernels
1 teaspoon salt
Black pepper
½ cup sour cream or plain lowfat
  yogurt, for garnish

1. In a large nonreactive soup pot or saucepan, warm 2 teaspoons of the corn oil over moderate heat. Add the onions and sauté until soft and lightly colored, 3 to 5 minutes. Add the garlic and cook for 1 minute longer. Stir in the tomatoes (no need to peel), cumin, chili powder, bay leaf and oregano. Coarsely chop 3 of the tortillas. Add the tortillas to the pot along with the tomato sauce, sugar, chicken stock and chicken breast. Bring to a boil over moderate heat, stirring once in awhile. Reduce the heat and simmer until the chicken is just cooked through, 4 to 5 minutes. Remove and let cool. Continue to simmer the soup for 25 to 30 minutes longer. Allow to cool slightly.

2. Remove the bay leaf. Working in batches, purée the soup in a blender or food processor. Strain back into the pot. Add the corn kernels and bring back to a boil. Remove from the heat. Stir in the salt and a pinch of pepper.

3. Meanwhile, use the remaining 1 teaspoon oil to coat a small heavy skillet set over a moderately-high flame. Stack the remaining 3 tortillas and cut them into four strips. Cut the strips crosswise into ¼-inch slivers. Turn them into the hot oil and brown well, stirring frequently, until crisp and golden brown. Drain on paper towels. Tear the chicken breast into fine shreds.

4. Spoon the soup into 6 shallow soup bowls. Divide the tortilla and shredded chicken among them. Add 1 tablespoon of the sour cream to each. Serve hot.

Calories 211 *Protein* 9 gm *Fat* 8 gm *Carbohydrate* 27 gm *Sodium* 405 mg *Cholesterol* 19 mg

CREAMY MUSHROOM SOUP
Here is a creamy mushroom soup with a good deep mushroom flavor, made even more delicious with a hint of lemon and a dab of cream cheese. If you want a thicker soup, dissolve 1 to 2 tablespoons cornstarch (29 calories per tablespoon) in cold water, stir in and simmer for an extra minute or two.

MAKES 6 SERVINGS OF
1 CUP EACH

1 tablespoon butter
1 medium (4-ounce) onion, finely
    chopped
1 small garlic clove, minced or crushed
    through a press
1 pound fresh mushrooms, cut into
    1/4-inch dice
1/4 cup all-purpose flour
3 cups chicken stock (recipe follows) or
    canned broth
1 cup milk
1/4 cup dry sherry
1 bay leaf, or 1/2 California bay
    laurel leaf
1/4 cup (2 ounces) cream cheese, cut into
    bits, at room temperature
1 tablespoon fresh lemon juice
1/4 teaspoon Tabasco sauce
3/4 teaspoon salt

1. Melt the butter in a heavy medium saucepan or soup pot over moderate heat. Add the onion and sauté until softened, 3 to 5 minutes. Add the garlic and cook for 30 seconds longer. Stir in the mushrooms and sauté, stirring frequently, over moderately-high heat until the mushrooms release their juices, 3 to 4 minutes. Sprinkle on the flour and stir to blend; cook for 1 minute longer. Add the chicken stock, milk and sherry. Stirring constantly, bring to a boil over moderate heat. Add the bay leaf and simmer over low heat for 15 minutes to blend the flavors. Stir in the cream cheese, lemon juice and Tabasco. Stir until smooth and the cream cheese has melted, about 2 minutes. Season with salt to taste; discard the bay leaf. Serve hot.

NOTE: One of the mushrooms can be thinly sliced and sautéed and reserved for garnish, especially if serving at a dinner party or for entertaining.

Calories *147*   **Protein** *5 gm*   **Fat** *8 gm*   **Carbohydrate** *16 gm*   **Sodium** *350 mg*   **Cholesterol** *21 mg*

CHICKEN STOCK *The great thing about making stock from scratch is that you don't have to add salt unless you want to and the flavor will be deeper, better and stronger than canned versions.*

MAKES 3 QUARTS OR 12 SERVINGS OF 1 CUP EACH

5 pounds chicken backs, necks, wing tips, bones, etc.
2 medium (4-ounce) onions, sliced
2 medium carrots, sliced
2 medium celery ribs, sliced
2 garlic cloves, sliced
1 large parsley sprig
½ teaspoon dried thyme
1 bay leaf

1. Combine all of the ingredients in a large stockpot or Dutch oven and add 4 quarts of cold water. Bring to a boil over moderate heat. Lower the heat to maintain a simmer and cook, skimming any foam that rises to the surface, stirring occasionally, for 4 hours.

2. Strain through a colander. Discard the solids. Strain through a fine sieve or a sieve lined with a double layer of dampened cheesecloth. Let cool to room temperature. You can skim the fat from the surface right away and use the degreased stock, or you can chill it and easily remove all the fat after it has solidified.

Calories *42*   **Protein** *1 gm*   **Fat** *2 gm*   **Carbohydrate** *6 gm*   **Sodium** *4 mg*   **Cholesterol** *0 mg*

MINESTRONE

If you like pasta in your minestrone, cook small elbow macaroni separately and add some to each serving (dried pasta contains 105 calories per ounce). You can also sprinkle each serving with a teaspoon of grated Parmesan cheese (10 calories) and you can substitute water for the chicken broth to make a purely vegetarian version of this soup.

*MAKES 12 SERVINGS OF
1 CUP EACH*

1 tablespoon olive oil
2 medium (4-ounce) onions, chopped
*2 medium carrots, peeled and cut into
    ½-inch dice (about 1 cup)*
*2 medium celery ribs, cut into ½-inch
    dice (about 1 cup)*
*1 large garlic clove, minced or crushed
    through a press*
*3 medium (4-ounce) red potatoes, peeled
    and cut into ½-inch dice*
*1 can (14½-ounce) whole peeled
    tomatoes, including juice, cut up*
*4 cups chicken stock (page 31) or
    canned broth*
1 bay leaf
*2 medium (6-ounce) zucchini, cut into
    ½-inch dice*
½ teaspoon dried basil, crumbled
½ teaspoon dried oregano, crumbled
*1 can (10½-ounce) red kidney beans,
    drained*
*1 can (10½-ounce) white kidney beans,
    drained*
½ cup drained, canned garbanzo beans
¼ cup dry white wine
¼ cup chopped Italian flat-leaf parsley
1½ teaspoons salt
Pepper

1. Spoon the olive oil into a large non-reactive saucepan or soup pot set over moderate heat. Add the onions, carrots and celery and sauté until slightly softened, about 3 minutes. Add the garlic and cook for 1 minute longer. Stir in the potatoes, the tomatoes and their juices, the chicken stock, 4 cups of water and the bay leaf. Bring to a boil over moderate heat, stirring occasionally. Reduce the heat and simmer for 30 minutes, stirring once in awhile.

2. Add the zucchini, basil and oregano; simmer for 10 minutes. Add the red and white kidney beans and the garbanzo beans and cook for 10 minutes longer. Remove from the heat. Stir in white wine and parsley. Season with salt and pepper to taste; discard the bay leaf. Serve hot, with grated Parmesan, if desired.

Calories 122   *Protein* 5 gm   *Fat* 2 gm   *Carbohydrate* 22 gm   *Sodium* 548 mg   *Cholesterol* 0 mg

VEGETARIAN CHILI *Rich, tasty and nutritious, too, this chili is a beautiful terra-cotta color, accented with a topping of Cheddar cheese, sliced scallions and sour cream. Make the chili a day before you want to serve it because it improves upon standing. For chopping vegetables in this quantity, I strongly recommend using a food processor.*

*MAKES 12 SERVINGS OF
1 CUP EACH*

8 ounces (½ package) dried small red
  beans, rinsed and picked over to
  remove any grit, or 3 cups drained
  and rinsed canned red beans
1 tablespoon vegetable oil
3 medium onions (1 pound), chopped
3 large celery ribs, cut into ¼-inch dice
  (2 cups)
¼ cup minced garlic
3 large carrots, finely chopped (2 cups)
2 cups packed, finely chopped cabbage
  (½ pound)
½ pound mushrooms, finely chopped
  (2 cups)
2 medium (4-ounce) red bell peppers,
  finely chopped (2 cups)
2 medium (4-ounce) green bell peppers,
  finely chopped (2 cups)
⅓ cup chili powder
1 tablespoon unsweetened cocoa powder
1 tablespoon sugar
1 tablespoon whole cumin seeds
1 tablespoon plus ¼ teaspoon dried
  oregano, crumbled
2 teaspoons whole fennel seeds
1 teaspoon dried thyme, crumbled
½ teaspoon cayenne pepper
½ teaspoon ground cinnamon
2 teaspoons salt
½ teaspoon black pepper

1 can (28-ounce) whole tomatoes,
  including juice
2 tablespoons soy sauce
2 tablespoons dry sherry
1 teaspooon Tabasco sauce or
  hot pepper sauce
*TOPPINGS FOR EACH 1 CUP
SERVING:*
  2 tablespoons sour cream
  2 tablespoons sliced scallion
  2 tablespoons shredded mild Cheddar
    cheese

1. If using dried beans, put the beans in a medium bowl and add enough cold water to cover by 3 inches. Let soak overnight; drain. (Alternatively, place the dried beans in a medium saucepan and add enough water to cover by 2 inches. Bring to a boil and cook for 1 minute. Remove from the heat, cover and let stand for 1 hour.) Place the beans in a medium saucepan and add enough water to cover by 3 inches. Bring to a boil over moderate heat. Reduce the heat and simmer until tender, about 1 hour; drain.

2. In a large nonreactive soup pot or casserole, warm the oil over moderate heat. Add the onions and celery and sauté until the onions are softened and translucent, 6 to 8 minutes. Add the garlic and cook for 1 minute longer.

3. Add the carrots, cabbage and mushrooms to the casserole and cook, stirring occasionally, until tender, about 10 minutes. Add the red and green peppers and cook until softened, 5 to 8 minutes.
4. Stir in the chili powder, cocoa, sugar, cumin seeds, 1 tablespoon oregano, fennel seeds, thyme, cayenne, cinnamon, salt and ¼ teaspoon of the black pepper. Stir in the tomatoes (including juice), breaking them up with a spoon, along with 4 cups of water. Add the soaked dried beans (see NOTE) and simmer over low heat, stirring occasionally, until

thick and rich tasting, about 2 hours. Remove from the heat; let cool to room temperature. Cover and refrigerate overnight.
5. Reheat the chili over low heat. Add the remaining ¼ teaspoon each of oregano and black pepper. Remove from the heat and stir in the soy sauce, sherry and Tabasco sauce. Serve the chili hot, topped with sour cream, scallions and Cheddar cheese.
NOTE: If using canned beans, add them after removing from the heat but before cooling to room temperature.

Calories 278   *Protein* 12 gm   *Fat* 14 gm   *Carbohydrate* 31 gm   *Sodium* 816 mg   *Cholesterol* 28 mg

---

CHILE VERDE
This Mexican green chile stew is usually made with more meat and fat. Poblano chiles, the mildest of chiles (they're just a step up the fire ladder from bell peppers), are doubled up here and I have used lean beef instead of the traditional marbled pork. Serve it in bowls with corn tortillas (40 to 50 calories each) or with 7-inch flour tortillas (about 100 calories each). You can also make this chile verde into succulent burritos or tacos. I suppose you could substitute canned, roasted, peeled chiles, but the salt content will be higher and the flavor not as good. This dish is excellent when served with Spanish Rice Timbales (page 121).

*MAKES 10 SERVINGS OF
1 CUP EACH*

*2 pounds trimmed lean beef round or
    sirloin, cut into ¾-inch cubes*
¼ cup all-purpose flour

*2 tablespoons plus 1 teaspoon vegetable
    oil*
4 medium (4-ounce) onions
*3 large garlic cloves, minced or crushed
    through a press*
2 teaspoons dried oregano, crumbled

1 teaspoon ground cumin
½ teaspoon dried thyme, crumbled
1 bay leaf
*1 can (14½-ounce) whole peeled
    tomatoes, with their juice*
½ cup canned tomato sauce
*4 pounds (18 to 24 medium-large) fresh
    green poblano chile peppers*
1½ teaspoons salt
¼ teaspoon black pepper

1. Shake half of the beef cubes in a bag with 2 tablespoons of the flour. Spoon 1 tablespoon of the vegetable oil into a large nonstick pot or nonreactive Dutch oven and place over moderately-high heat. Add the floured beef and brown well, without stirring, for 3 to 5 minutes; turn the pieces of beef and brown for 2 to 3 minutes longer. With a slotted spoon, transfer the meat to a bowl. Repeat with the remaining beef, flour and 1 tablespoon of the remaining oil.

2. Trim the ends from the onions and halve them lengthwise. Peel; slice crosswise into thin slices. Add the remaining 1 teaspoon oil to the pan along with the onions. Sauté over moderate heat until softened and lightly colored, about 5 minutes, adding 1 to 2 tablespoons of water each time the onions seem dry. Add the garlic and cook for 1 minute longer. Return the beef, along with any accumulated juices, and stir in the oregano, cumin, thyme, bay leaf, tomatoes and their juice and the tomato sauce. Break up the tomatoes with a spoon. Bring the mixture to a boil over moderate heat. Cover, reduce the heat and simmer gently, stirring occasionally, for 1½ hours, until the meat is tender.

3. Meanwhile, roast the poblano peppers directly over a gas flame or under the broiler as close to the heat as possible, turning until blistered and charred black all over. Place the peppers in a large plastic bag, twist the top to enclose, and cool for 15 minutes. Working over a colander, peel the peppers by rubbing their skins gently under running warm water. Pull out the stems and ribs and rinse off the seeds. Tear the chiles, lengthwise, into ¼ to ½-inch wide strips.

4. Add the chiles, salt and pepper to the stew. Simmer for about 30 minutes longer, until the beef is tender. Serve hot. **(This recipe can be prepared entirely ahead of time and refrigerated for 3 or 4 days. Reheat to serve.)**

NOTE: Poblano chiles are the mildest of chiles, but once in awhile a fire-hot one can be found. Wear rubber gloves when working with them, since their oils can irritate the eyes and skin.

Calories 232   *Protein 23 gm*   *Fat 8 gm*   *Carbohydrate 17 gm*   *Sodium 530 mg*   *Cholesterol 53 mg*

CHUNKY FISH CHOWDER *Chunks of codfish and potato in a thick, creamy chowder flavored with smoky bacon make a comforting supper dish.*

MAKES 6 SERVINGS

*3 slices lean smoked bacon, cut into
  ¹/₂-inch squares (3 ounces)*
1 cup milk
1 bottle (8-ounce) clam juice
1 cup diced celery
1 medium (4-ounce) onion, chopped
1 medium carrot, peeled and chopped
*2 medium (6-ounce) boiling potatoes,
  peeled and cut into 1-inch pieces*
1 large garlic clove, minced
1 bay leaf
¹/₂ teaspoon dried basil, crumbled
¹/₈ teaspoon dried thyme, crumbled
2 tablespoons all-purpose flour
*1 pound fresh cod fillets, cut into 1-inch
  chunks*
¹/₂ teaspoon salt
¹/₄ teaspoon black pepper
¹/₄ cup chopped parsley
Lemon slices, for garnish

1. Fry the bacon in a small skillet over moderate heat until crisp and golden, about 5 minutes. Drain on paper towels.
2. In a large nonreactive saucepan or casserole, combine the milk and clam juice with 1 cup water. Add the celery, onion, carrot, potatoes, garlic, bay leaf, basil, thyme and bacon. Bring to a boil over moderate heat, stirring occasionally. With a fork, quickly stir the flour into 1 cup water until blended and smooth. Stir the mixture into the soup and return to a boil. Reduce the heat to low and simmer until the potatoes are very tender, 20 to 30 minutes.
3. Add the cod and simmer until just opaque throughout, about 5 minutes. Stir in the salt, pepper and parsley. Discard the bay leaf. Serve hot in soup plates. Garnish with lemon slices.

Calories *171*   **Protein** *18 gm*   **Fat** *4 gm*   **Carbohydrate** *15 gm*   **Sodium** *418 mg*   **Cholesterol** *42 mg*

36

NEW ENGLAND CLAM CHOWDER *Here is a rich and creamy clam chowder. It is hearty fare, yet is made without the traditional butter and heavy cream. If you can't find fresh cherrystone or chowder clams, I suppose that you could start with canned clams and bottled clam juice, measure for measure, though fresh invariably produces tastier results and the canned products contain more salt.*

*MAKES 8 SERVINGS OF
1 CUP EACH*

*1 dozen large (3-inch) cherrystone or
   chowder clams
1 slice (1 ounce) lean smoked bacon, cut
   into ½-inch squares
1 large (6-ounce) onion, chopped
¼ teaspoon dried thyme, crumbled
¼ cup all-purpose flour
4 cups milk
2 large (8-ounce) baking potatoes, peeled
   and cut into ½-inch cubes
1 tablespoon cornstarch
½ teaspoon Worcestershire sauce
   (optional)
⅛ teaspoon black pepper
Chopped parsley, for garnish*

1. Put the clams in a large bowl of cold water and scrub them with a brush. Rinse well. Put the clams in a large heavy pot and cover. Place over high heat and cook until they open, 4 to 5 minutes. Remove with tongs; let cool slightly. Reserve 1 cup of the clam juice.

2. With a small spoon, scoop the clams from their shells. Some may not be open all the way but can be easily pried open with a spoon or butter knife; discard any that cannot be easily pried open. If there is more than 1 cup of clam juice, discard some. If there is less, add water or bottled clam juice to make 1 cup. Reserve the whole clams in the juice until needed.

3. Put the bacon in a heavy large soup pot or saucepan and cook over moderate heat, stirring frequently, until crisp and golden brown, about 3 minutes. Add the onion and sauté until softened, 3 to 5 minutes. With a fork, stir in the thyme and flour. The flour will not dissolve completely in the small amount of fat but will moisten enough to dissolve when the liquid is added. Stir in the milk. Place over moderate heat and, stirring constantly, bring to a boil. Reduce the heat and simmer until thickened and creamy, about 3 minutes. Add the potatoes and bring to a boil. Reduce the heat, partially cover, and simmer, stirring once in awhile, until the potatoes are tender, about 15 minutes.

4. Remove the clams from the juice; reserve the juice and drain the clams. In a small bowl, dissolve the cornstarch in the clam juice. Pour into the soup and, stirring constantly, return to a boil. Cook until thickened. Reduce the heat to low.

5. Coarsely chop the clams (about 3 cuts lengthwise and then 4 crosswise) and add them to the chowder. Simmer for 2 to 3 minutes. Remove from the heat and add the Worcestershire sauce and pepper. Serve hot, with a pinch of chopped parsley.

NOTE: Clams sometimes give up more liquid after they are added. If not serving this chowder right away, you may want to dissolve 1 tablespoon cornstarch in 2 tablespoons water and stir in when reheating.

Calories 175   *Protein* 10 gm   *Fat* 7 gm   *Carbohydrate* 19 gm   *Sodium* 104 mg   *Cholesterol* 30 mg

SIDE-DISH & SUPPER SALADS

If you think of salads as diet-food nibbles, try feasting on these—fresh tuna salad with roasted sweet peppers, perhaps, or a mouthwatering Thai beef salad hot off the charcoal grill. You'll find cole slaw and two potato salads, indispensable to any picnic. And if you're used to doing without rich, creamy dressings, take a look at the recipes for bleu cheese or green goddess dressings, and enjoy.

Z APPY COLE SLAW *This intensely flavored salad will surely wake up even the most sluggish of taste buds. It is especially good when paired with the Sautéed Codfish Cakes on page 131.*

MAKES 4 SERVINGS

¼ cup plain lowfat yogurt
2 teaspoons Dijon mustard
½ teaspoon powdered mustard
½ teaspoon prepared white horseradish, drained
1 teaspoon sugar
¼ teaspoon celery seeds
¼ teaspoon salt
¼ teaspoon black pepper
1½ tablespoons fresh lemon juice
2 cups packed finely shredded green cabbage (about 6 ounces)

1. In a medium bowl, stir together the yogurt, Dijon mustard, powdered mustard, horseradish, sugar, celery seeds, salt, pepper and lemon juice. Add the cabbage and toss to coat. Refrigerate, stirring occasionally, for 2 to 3 hours. Serve cold.

Calories *30*   **Protein** *1 gm*   **Fat** *.5 gm*   **Carbohydrate** *5 gm*   **Sodium** *230 mg*   **Cholesterol** *1 mg*

TABBOULEH

T ABBOULEH *Most versions of the fragrant wheat and vegetable salad known as tabbouleh contain at least a half cup of olive oil. This version requires only 3 tablespoons for six servings. A logical addition to Middle Eastern menus, this salad is also perfect for salad parties, barbecues and lunch boxes.*

MAKES 6 SERVINGS OF
1 CUP EACH

¾ cup medium-grain bulghur wheat
  (5 ounces)
1 large cucumber
1 medium green bell pepper, trimmed
  and cut into ½-inch squares (1 cup)
2 large tomatoes, cut into ½-inch dice
  (2 cups)
1 cup thinly sliced scallions (8 to 12
  medium)
1 cup finely chopped parsley
½ cup finely chopped mint
¼ cup fresh lemon juice
3 tablespoons olive oil
¾ teaspoon salt
¼ teaspoon black pepper

1. Put the bulghur in a medium bowl and fill with lukewarm tap water. Pour off and discard the water, leaving the wheat behind in the bowl. Repeat twice more to clean the wheat. Fill the bowl with hot tap water and let the wheat soak for 30 minutes. Drain through a sieve, pressing to extract as much water as possible.
2. Peel the cucumber and trim the ends. Cut the cucumber in half lengthwise; scoop out the seeds and discard. Cut the halves lengthwise into ½-inch strips, and then crosswise into ½-inch dice. Turn into a large bowl. Add the bell pepper, tomatoes, scallions, parsley, mint, lemon juice, oil, salt and pepper. Toss together. Add the bulghur and toss again. Cover and refrigerate for at least 2 hours or up to 2 or 3 days. Serve cold.

Calories *181*   **Protein** *4 gm*   **Fat** *8 gm*   **Carbohydrate** *27 gm*   **Sodium** *288 mg*   **Cholesterol** *0 mg*

HOT GERMAN POTATO SALAD *This version of the classic favorite retains the flavor, but not the fat, of traditional recipes for this dish. Just a little bacon does the tasty trick.*

MAKES 6 SERVINGS

12 small new red potatoes (about
   1 pound)
2 slices smoked bacon (1¾-ounces), cut
   into ½-inch squares
1 cup finely diced celery
1 medium (4-ounce) onion, chopped
2 teaspoons all-purpose flour
2 teaspoons sugar
2 teaspoons German or brown mustard
⅛ teaspoon celery seeds
2 tablespoons cider vinegar
2 cups coarsely chopped romaine lettuce
   heart
2 tablespoons chopped parsley
Salt and pepper

1. Put the potatoes into a large pot of cold water. Cover and bring to a boil over high heat. Boil, partially covered, until tender when pierced with a fork, about 15 minutes. Drain and return to the hot pot. Fill a medium serving bowl with very hot or boiling water (you can drain the potato water into it as I do) to heat it.

2. Put the bacon in a large heavy skillet and cook, stirring, over moderate heat until crisp and golden brown, 2 to 3 minutes. Add the celery and onion and cook until hot but still crunchy, 1 to 2 minutes. Stir in the flour and cook, stirring, for 30 seconds. Stir in the sugar, mustard, celery seeds, vinegar and ⅓ cup water. Bring to a boil, stirring, until thickened. Add the romaine lettuce and remove from the heat.

3. Dump the hot water from the bowl and dry it. Working quickly, cut the potatoes (unpeeled) into quarters and put them in the hot bowl. Pour the hot dressing over and toss with the parsley and salt and pepper to taste. Serve right away.

Calories 132   *Protein* 3 gm   *Fat* 5 gm   *Carbohydrate* 19 gm   *Sodium* 133 mg   *Cholesterol* 6 mg

---

OLD-FASHIONED POTATO SALAD *Grandma was right. The early American-style boiled salad dressing, used instead of mayonnaise to make potato salad and cole slaw, may be the best choice of all. It is very low in fat and very tasty. Serve the salad the same day you make it.*

*MAKES 8 SERVINGS OF
1 CUP EACH*

1 tablespoon olive oil
2 tablespoons all-purpose flour
1 cup milk
*3 pounds red-skinned potatoes (10 to 12
   medium)*
*2 tablespoons golden or brown prepared
   mustard*
1 tablespoon cider vinegar
2 hard-cooked eggs, coarsely shredded
*½ cup thinly sliced scallions (4 to 6
   medium)*
¼ cup finely chopped parsley
¼ teaspoon black pepper
Salt
Parsley sprigs, for garnish

1. Spoon the oil into a small heavy saucepan and place over moderate heat. Add the flour and stir for 30 seconds. Pour in the milk and cook, stirring constantly, until it begins to boil and thicken. Reduce the heat and simmer for 1 minute. Turn into a large bowl and set aside to cool to room temperature, stirring occasionally.

2. Meanwhile, put the potatoes into a large pot and add cold water to cover by 1 inch. Cover and bring to a boil over high heat. Boil, partially covered, until tender when pierced with a fork, 30 to 40 minutes. Drain and let cool to room temperature.

3. Stir the mustard, vinegar, hard-cooked eggs, scallions, parsley and pepper into the boiled dressing. Season with salt to taste. Peel the potatoes (or leave unpeeled if desired) and cut them into 1-inch chunks, dropping them into the dressing as they are cut. Toss well. Cover and chill for 1 hour. Mound the salad onto a platter, and garnish with the parsley sprigs.

Calories 204   *Protein* 6 gm   *Fat* 5 gm   *Carbohydrate* 34 gm   *Sodium* 84 mg   *Cholesterol* 73 mg

BEAN SPROUT SALAD *I love Chinese bean sprouts. They can be crisp and cool and crunchy and are no trouble to prepare. Although you start with what seems like a huge amount, they shrink considerably after blanching and marinating.*

MAKES 8 SERVINGS OF
½ CUP EACH

2 pounds fresh bean sprouts, drained
3 tablespoons reduced-sodium soy sauce,
  or to taste
2 tablespoons Oriental sesame oil
2 tablespoons dry sherry
2 tablespoons rice vinegar, or
  1 tablespoon distilled white vinegar
¼ teaspoon hot pepper sauce
1 large (8-ounce) red bell pepper,
  trimmed and cut into 2-inch julienne

1. Bring a large pot of lightly salted water to a boil over high heat. Drop in the bean sprouts and cook for 1 minute. Drain in a colander and refresh under cold running water. Drain well.
2. In a large bowl, whisk together the soy sauce, sesame oil, sherry, vinegar and hot pepper sauce. Add the bean sprouts and bell pepper. Toss and serve cool, or refrigerate and serve cold.

Calories 80 **Protein** 4 gm **Fat** 4 gm **Carbohydrate** 9 gm **Sodium** 237 mg **Cholesterol** 0 mg

CUCUMBER-RADISH RAITA *This cool and refreshing cucumber salad is simple to put together and does well alongside spicy Indian dishes such as Beef with Spicy Spinach Sauce (page 164) or My Skinny Cheeseburgers (page 170).*

MAKES 8 SERVINGS OF
½ CUP EACH

3 large cucumbers
½ teaspoon salt
1 teaspoon ground cumin
¾ cup plain lowfat yogurt
¼ cup sour cream
¼ teaspoon black pepper
6 medium radishes, thinly sliced

1. Peel the cucumbers with a swivel-bladed vegetable peeler. Cut them in half lengthwise; scoop out the seeds with a spoon and discard. Cut the cucumbers crosswise into ¼-inch slices. Put them in a large colander and toss with ¼ teaspoon of the salt. Let drain for 1 hour. Rinse well, drain and pat dry on several layers of paper towels. Put in a large bowl.

2. Spoon the cumin into a small dry skillet and toast lightly, stirring or shaking over moderate heat, for about 30 seconds, until fragrant. Remove from the heat.

3. In a small bowl, whisk together the yogurt, sour cream, pepper and cumin. Pour over the cucumbers and toss to coat. Chill for 1 hour. Fold in the radishes. Serve cold.

Calories 43   *Protein* 2 gm   *Fat* 2 gm   *Carbohydrate* 5 gm   *Sodium* 159 mg   *Cholesterol* 4 mg

MOM'S MARINATED SALAD *My mother made this deliciously crunchy salad for most backyard barbecues after we moved to California. It makes a quantity large enough for a party, or can be simply kept in the refrigerator all week, to be enjoyed every day.*

*MAKES 12 SERVINGS OF
1 CUP EACH*

2 cups small cauliflower florets, cut into tiny pieces or chopped

4 medium carrots, peeled, thinly sliced and quartered (1½ cups)

2 medium zucchini, thinly sliced and quartered (1½ cups)

1 medium green bell pepper, trimmed and cut into ½-inch squares (1 cup)

½ pound green beans, trimmed and cut into ½-inch lengths (1½ cups)

2 cups purple cabbage, finely chopped

1 cup diced celery

3 to 4 medium tomatoes (about 1 pound), cut into ½-inch dice (2 cups)

8 medium radishes, thinly sliced and quartered (1 cup)

½ cup thinly sliced scallions

½ cup rice vinegar

¼ cup olive oil

1½ teaspoons salt

½ teaspoon black pepper

1½ teaspoons dried basil, crumbled

1 teaspoon dried oregano, crumbled

½ teaspoon dried thyme, crumbled

1 tablespoon paprika

¼ teaspoon cayenne pepper (optional)

1. In a large bowl, combine cauliflower, carrots, zucchini, bell pepper, green beans, cabbage, celery, tomatoes, radishes and scallions. Toss to mix evenly.

2. In a medium bowl, whisk together the vinegar, oil, salt, black pepper, basil, oregano, thyme, paprika and cayenne. Pour the dressing over the vegetables and toss to coat. Transfer to a bowl just large enough to hold the salad. Cover and refrigerate for at least 2 hours, or as long as 4 or 5 days. Serve cold.

Calories *81*　**Protein** *2 gm*　**Fat** *5 gm*　**Carbohydrate** *9 gm*　**Sodium** *303 mg*　**Cholesterol** *0 mg*

ARTICHOKE-RICE SALAD *Although I have called for dried herbs here, if fresh ones are available, by all means use them. This large salad is festive and colorful, perfect for parties. The reddish-purple radicchio (optional), yellow lemons, bright orange carrots and green parsley make it an edible rainbow.*

MAKES 10 SERVINGS
OF SLIGHTLY MORE THAN
1 CUP EACH

6 medium, firm artichokes (2 pounds)
3 lemons
1 cup long-grain white rice
3 tablespoons olive oil
2 medium (3-ounce) carrots, peeled and
   cut into ¼-inch dice
1 large cucumber, peeled, halved
   lengthwise, seeded and cut into
   ½-inch dice
1 cup finely diced celery
½ cup thinly sliced scallions
¼ cup chopped parsley, preferably flat-
   leaf Italian
Salt and pepper

DRESSING:

2 teaspoons cornstarch
½ cup canned chicken broth or stock
2 tablespoons cider vinegar
1 teaspoon dried basil, crumbled
½ teaspoon dried oregano, crumbled
1 tablespoon olive oil
8 to 12 radicchio leaves (optional) or
   small romaine lettuce leaves
Parsley sprigs, for garnish

1. Slice off about 1 inch from the top of each artichoke. Cut one of the lemons in half and rub the cut surfaces of the artichokes with lemon. Cut the remaining 2½ lemons into wedges for serving. Trim the artichoke stems so that there is only 1 inch on each. Pull off all of the tough outer leaves, leaving only the pale green tender ones toward the center. Rub all of the surfaces with lemon and put the artichokes in a large pot of cold water; add that lemon half to the water. Cover and bring to a boil over high heat. Boil, partially covered, until tender when pierced with a fork, about 15 minutes. Remove and drain upside down. Let cool.

2. Bring a medium pot of water to a boil. Slowly add the rice grains so the boiling doesn't stop. Boil until tender but slightly firm, 12 to 14 minutes. Add 1 cup of cold water to stop the cooking; drain well. Turn the rice into a large bowl; add the oil and toss. Let cool thoroughly, stirring once in awhile. Add the carrots, cucumber, celery, scallions, parsley and salt and pepper to taste. Toss.

3. With a small spoon, scoop out the fuzzy choke from the center of each artichoke. Working lengthwise, cut the artichokes into wedges, about ½-inch wide (each wedge will contain stem, heart and center leaves). Add to the salad and toss. Chill briefly.

4. PREPARE THE DRESSING: In a small nonreactive saucepan, dissolve the cornstarch in the chicken broth. Stir in the vinegar, basil and oregano. Place over moderate heat and, stirring constantly, bring to a boil, stirring until thickened. Remove from the heat and stir in the oil. Allow to cool slightly.

5. To serve, ring the edge of a large platter with the radicchio leaves or line with romaine leaves. Mound the salad in the center, and pour the dressing over the top. Serve cool.

Calories 152	**Protein** 3 gm	**Fat** 6 gm	**Carbohydrate** 23 gm	**Sodium** 98 mg	**Cholesterol** 0 mg

CHICKEN SUPPER SALAD
Here is a hearty main-dish salad, a close relative of the classic chef's salad but dressed lightly, without all the calories of a traditional oil and vinegar dressing. Prepare the Herb Vinaigrette on page 55 ahead of time and let it cool.

MAKES 4 SERVINGS

½ pound (1 small) whole skinless boned chicken breast, split
½ pound tender young green beans, ends trimmed
3 medium carrots, thinly sliced
2 medium inner celery ribs, thinly sliced on an angle
1 large cucumber, peeled
1 medium (4-ounce) red bell pepper, quartered lengthwise
1 medium-large (8-ounce) zucchini, ends trimmed
½ pint (1 generous cup) small cherry tomatoes, halved
⅔ cup Herb Vinaigrette (page 55)
8 cups romaine lettuce leaves, torn up
4 cups fresh spinach leaves, torn up
4 thin slices lean ham (3 ounces), cut into ¼-by-2-inch-strips
½ cup Swiss cheese, cut in ¼-by-2-inch julienne (2 ounces)
Salt and pepper
2 lemons, each cut into 4 wedges

1. Put the chicken in a small skillet or saucepan with ¾ cup cold water. Place over moderate heat, cover, and bring to a boil. Lower the heat and simmer just until cooked through, 10 to 12 minutes. Remove from the water; let cool to room temperature. If making ahead, wrap in plastic and chill.

2. Bring a medium pot of water to a boil. Add a pinch of salt and the beans. Return to the boil and cook just until tender, 3 to 5 minutes. Rinse under cold water and drain.

3. In a medium bowl, toss together the carrots and celery. Cut the cucumber lengthwise in half and scoop out the seeds with a small spoon; discard. Cut the cucumber crosswise into ¼-inch slices and add to the bowl. Cut out the stems and ribs from the bell pepper quarters and tap out the seeds. Cut into ¼-inch strips and add to the bowl. Cut the zucchini lengthwise in half and then crosswise into thin half rounds; add to the bowl along with the cherry tomato halves. Pour all of the dressing over the salad and toss to coat the ingredients. **(This can be prepared several hours ahead and refrigerated.)**

4. To assemble the salads: put 2 cups of the romaine into each of 4 large individual salad bowls (or on dinner plates) and top each with 1 cup spinach. Toss. Spoon one-fourth of the marinated vegetables over each, drizzling equal amounts of any dressing in the bottom of the bowl over each salad. Arrange one-fourth of the green beans in a bunch at the side of each salad. Tear the chicken, in the direction of the grain, into shreds and place one-fourth in the center of each salad. Scatter equal amounts of ham and Swiss cheese over each. Sprinkle with salt and pepper to taste. Add 2 lemon wedges to each bowl. To eat, squeeze one lemon wedge over the chicken and the other over the green beans.

Calories 286   *Protein* 28 gm   *Fat* 10 gm   *Carbohydrate* 24 gm   *Sodium* 625 mg   *Cholesterol* 56 mg

---

CHINESE CHICKEN SALAD

Here is a large special salad for sensible, healthy entertaining. It is beautiful with its various shades and tones of green and yellow-green, set off by lemon yellow. If available, use fresh water chestnuts (page 150) because their flavor and texture are far superior to the canned versions. The only oil in this salad is a tablespoon of Oriental sesame oil, used specifically for its toasted nutty flavor.

*MAKES 12 SERVINGS OF
1½ CUPS EACH*

1 pound skinless boned chicken breast
  halves
½ cup plus 2 tablespoons dry sherry
3 slices fresh ginger, each the size of a
  quarter
5 medium scallions, thinly sliced (set 1
  aside)
1 large garlic clove, sliced
1 pound fresh water chestnuts, peeled,
  or 2 cans (8-ounce) sliced water
  chestnuts, drained
1 tablespoon fresh lemon juice
1 pound fresh green beans, ends trimmed
  and beans halved lengthwise between
  the seams
2 pounds fresh bean sprouts
½ pound fresh mushrooms, sliced slightly
  less than ¼-inch thick
2 teaspoons cornstarch
3 tablespoons rice vinegar
2 tablespoons soy sauce
1 tablespoon Oriental sesame oil

⅓ cup shredded fresh ginger
6 cups lightly packed shredded Napa
  cabbage (10 ounces)
2 bunches fresh watercress, coarse stems
  removed (4 cups)
1 teaspoon salt
¼ teaspoon black pepper
2 lemons, each cut into 6 wedges

1. Put the chicken breast halves in a medium skillet. Add ¼ cup of water, ½ cup of the sherry, the sliced ginger, 1 of the scallions and the garlic. Bring just to a boil over moderate heat. Reduce the heat to low, cover the pan, and simmer, turning 2 or 3 times, until just cooked through, 10 to 12 minutes. Remove the chicken from the poaching liquid; cover and let cool to room temperature. Strain the poaching liquid; you should have about ⅓ cup. Reserve it for the dressing.
2. Bring a medium pot of water to a boil over high heat. If there are any brown spots on the water chestnuts, cut them out. Add the water chestnuts and the lemon juice to the water and boil over moderate heat until tender, about 8 minutes. Drain and put the water chestnuts in a bowl of cold water. Drain and slice crosswise ⅛ inch thick. If using canned water chestnuts, simply drain and toss with the lemon juice.

3. Bring a large pot of lightly salted water to a boil over high heat. Drop in the green beans and cook just until tender, 2 to 3 minutes. Scoop out with a slotted spoon and drain further. Return the water to the boil and drop in the bean sprouts and mushrooms. Cook for exactly 1 minute from the time they went in. Drain and rinse under cold water. Let drain further.

4. Add enough cold water to the reserved poaching liquid (chicken) to make ½ cup. Stir in the cornstarch until dissolved. Pour the mixture into a small nonreactive saucepan along with the remaining 2 tablespoons sherry, the rice vinegar and soy sauce. Stirring constantly, bring to a boil over moderate heat. Simmer for a minute, to thicken slightly. Remove from the heat and stir in the sesame oil. Wrap the shredded ginger in a double layer of cheesecloth and squeeze over a bowl to wring out 1 tablespoon of ginger juice. Add the juice to the dressing.

5. With your fingers, tear the chicken into coarse shreds. In a large bowl, combine the cabbage, watercress, remaining 4 scallions, the water chestnuts, green beans, bean sprouts, mushrooms and chicken. Pour the dressing over the salad. Season with the salt and pepper. Toss to coat with dressing. Arrange the salad on a large oval platter; decorate the edge with lemon wedges. Serve right away.

Calories 134 *Protein* 13 gm *Fat* 2 gm *Carbohydrate* 18 gm *Sodium* 399 mg *Cholesterol* 22 mg

---

FRESH TUNA SALAD WITH ROASTED RED, YELLOW AND GREEN PEPPERS

There is nothing quite as special as fresh tuna (which bears little resemblance to canned versions). In this elegant salad, the sweetness of the roasted peppers punctuates the slight bite from the watercress and Belgian endive very nicely indeed. Use the white wine served with dinner to make the dressing. Serve the salad warm or at room temperature.

MAKES 8 SERVINGS OF
1 CUP EACH

1 large (8-ounce) red bell pepper
1 large (8-ounce) yellow bell pepper
1 large (8-ounce) green bell pepper
2 medium (3-ounce) heads of Belgian
    endive
2 bunches watercress, coarse stems
    removed
4 medium scallions, thinly sliced
2 tablespoons capers, with a little of the
    brine
1 tablespoon Dijon mustard
2 tablespoons mayonnaise
1 to 2 tablespoons fresh lemon juice
1½ tablespoons olive oil
1½ pounds fresh tuna steaks (de-boned
    and skinned), cut into ¾-inch cubes
2 tablespoons dry white wine
Salt and pepper

1. Roast the red, yellow and green peppers directly over a gas flame or under the broiler as close to the heat as possible, turning until charred all over. Put them in a plastic bag, twisting the top to enclose and let steam for 5 minutes in the refrigerator. Working over a colander, peel the peppers by rubbing the skins gently under warm running water. Remove the cores and seeds; cut the peppers into strips about ¼-inch wide and 3-inches long.

2. Cut the endive lengthwise into ¼-inch shreds. In a large bowl, toss the endive with the watercress, scallions, and peppers.

3. In a small bowl, combine the capers and mustard; mash with a fork. Stir in the mayonnaise and 1 tablespoon of the lemon juice.

4. Spoon the oil into a large nonstick skillet and place over moderately high heat. Add the tuna cubes and stir-fry until almost cooked through but just slightly rare inside (do not overcook), about 2 minutes. Spoon onto the salad and pour the wine over the tuna. Add the dressing and toss quickly. Add salt and pepper to taste. Serve warm or at room temperature, adding an additional tablespoon of lemon juice if desired (use sparingly when serving a good wine).

Calories 190   *Protein* 21 gm   *Fat* 10 gm   *Carbohydrate* 4 gm   *Sodium* 184 mg   *Cholesterol* 34 mg

THAI BEEF SALAD

THAI BEEF SALAD *Though not exactly the traditional way to prepare a classic Thai salad (I have substituted anchovies, ginger juice and oyster sauce for the slightly difficult to find Thai fish sauce), this version is perhaps even more delicious. Chinese oyster sauce can be purchased in most supermarkets nowadays. Both mint and cilantro (fresh coriander) are called for, but either can be used alone. Note that the beef should marinate for 4 to 8 hours or more and it can be broiled over charcoal or under the broiler.*

*MAKES 4 MAIN-COURSE
SERVINGS OR 8 SALAD SERVINGS*

1 pound lean flank steak, in one piece
2 teaspoons anchovy paste
1 tablespoon fresh ginger juice (see NOTE)
2 tablespoons Chinese oyster sauce
1 tablespoon peanut or vegetable oil
1 medium garlic clove, minced or crushed through a press
3 medium, fresh jalapeño chile peppers, seeded, deribbed and minced (3 tablespoons), for a hotter result, leave some of the seeds in.
Pinch of salt
1 tablespoon sugar
¼ cup fresh lime juice
1 small head (8- to 10-ounce) romaine lettuce
½ medium (4-ounce) red onion, slivered lengthwise
1 medium-large (4-ounce) firm head of Belgian endive, cored and slivered lengthwise
1 large cucumber, peeled, halved lengthwise, seeded and cut into ¼-inch slices
4 medium scallions, quartered lengthwise and cut into 1-inch lengths
¼ cup chopped mint

¼ cup chopped cilantro (fresh coriander)
½ teaspoon coarsely cracked black pepper or red hot pepper flakes to taste

NOTE: To make 1 tablespoon ginger juice, place ¼ to ⅓ cup (this depends on its freshness and juiciness) shredded fresh ginger (no need to peel) on a double layer of damp cheesecloth. Wring out over a bowl.

1. Prick the steak all over on both sides with a fork. In a small bowl, stir together the anchovy paste, ginger juice, 1 tablespoon of the oyster sauce and the oil. Pour into a shallow glass dish or zip-lock bag; add the beef. Let marinate in the refrigerator, turning once or twice for 4 to 8 hours. Let come to room temperature for about 30 minutes before broiling.

2. Meanwhile, prepare the dressing: Combine the garlic, jalapeños and salt in a small bowl. Pound with a pestle or the bottom of a spice jar to make a watery paste. Stir in the remaining 1 tablespoon oyster sauce, the sugar and lime juice.

3. Start a charcoal fire or preheat the broiler. Broil the beef to the medium stage, or to taste, 4 to 5 minutes per side. Remove and wrap in aluminum foil until needed.

4. Cut the romaine leaves in half lengthwise and arrange on a large serving platter. Scatter the onion and endive slivers over the lettuce. Ring the edge of the platter with the cucumber slices. Sprinkle the salad with the scallions, mint and cilantro. Take the steak from the foil, reserving juices, and thinly slice across the grain, halving the strips if they are long. Arrange the beef over the salad and pour the dressing and any meat juices over the top. Sprinkle with the cracked pepper or red pepper flakes and serve.

NOTE: Nutritional values given below refer to a single, main-course serving.

Calories 291	*Protein* 27 gm	*Fat* 15 gm	*Carbohydrate* 14 gm	*Sodium* 596 mg	*Cholesterol* 58 mg

CREAMY "MAYONNAISE" DRESSING *No oil is used here. Instead, fresh tofu is emulsified with an egg, and the resulting dressing resembles mayonnaise. It is good with Shrimp Sausages (page 19), on sandwiches or as a dip for vegetables.*

MAKES 1 CUP OR 16 SERVINGS OF 1 TABLESPOON EACH

1 cake (6 ounces) fresh tofu, cut up
1 large egg
¼ cup freshly grated Parmesan cheese
  (1 ounce)
½ teaspoon dried basil, crumbled
¼ teaspoon dried oregano, crumbled
½ teaspoon salt
⅛ teaspoon black pepper
1 tablespoon fresh lemon juice

1. In a food processor or blender, combine the tofu, egg, Parmesan, basil, oregano, salt and pepper. Process to a purée. Add the lemon juice and process for 30 seconds to 1 minute, until smooth. Cover and store in the refrigerator or use right away.

NOTE: Nutritional values given below refer to a single tablespoon serving.

Calories 20	*Protein* 2 gm	*Fat* 1 gm	*Carbohydrate* .5 gm	*Sodium* 102 mg	*Cholesterol* 18 mg

HERB VINAIGRETTE *This low-calorie, lowfat salad dressing is wonderfully sharp and sour. For variety, change the herbs to suit your taste; to decrease tartness, eliminate either the lemon juice or vinegar. To remove the trace of heat, you can forgo the cayenne pepper.*

MAKES ⅔ CUP OR 10 SERVINGS OF 1 TABLESPOON EACH

1 teaspoon cornstarch
1 tablespoon fresh lemon juice
1 tablespoon wine- or cider vinegar
½ teaspoon dried basil, crumbled
¼ teaspoon dried oregano, crumbled
¼ teaspoon paprika
⅛ teaspoon cayenne pepper
¼ teaspoon salt
⅛ teaspoon black pepper
1 tablespoon olive oil

1. In a small nonreactive saucepan, stir together ½ cup of water with the cornstarch, lemon juice and vinegar until the cornstarch dissolves. Stir in the basil, oregano, paprika, cayenne, salt and black pepper. Place over moderate heat and, stirring or whisking constantly, bring to a boil. Lower the heat and simmer for 30 seconds. Remove from the heat and stir in the olive oil. Let cool to room temperature. Use right away or cover and refrigerate for up to a week. **NOTE:** Nutritional values given below refer to a single tablespoon serving.

Calories 14	**Protein** 0 gm	**Fat** 1 gm	**Carbohydrate** .5 gm	**Sodium** 54 mg	**Cholesterol** 0 mg

BLEU CHEESE DRESSING *I like this sharp and creamy dressing over romaine lettuce hearts with chopped ripe tomato and cucumber. One-quarter cup of the dressing is enough for a generous 2-cup salad. You may substitute yogurt for the sour cream if desired. It is also tasty on potatoes or potato skins.*

MAKES 1 CUP OR 16 SERVINGS OF 1 TABLESPOON EACH

3 ounces Bleu cheese (about ⅓ cup packed)

½ cup plain lowfat yogurt
⅓ cup sour cream (or plain lowfat yogurt)
Salt and pepper

1. Crumble the Bleu cheese in a small bowl and mash in the yogurt with a fork. Stir in the sour cream. Season with salt and pepper to taste. Use right away, or cover and refrigerate for up to 5 days or so.

NOTE: Nutritional values given below refer to a single tablespoon serving.

Calories 33	Protein 2 gm	Fat 3 gm	Carbohydrate 1 gm	Sodium 82 mg	Cholesterol 7 mg

THOUSAND ISLAND DRESSING *Made with a mere fraction of the fat that most versions of this classic dressing contain, this one is delicious on salads and is good spooned into avocados or over hamburgers and sandwiches.*

MAKES 1¼ CUPS OR 20 SERVINGS OF 1 TABLESPOON EACH

⅓ cup sour cream
¼ cup plain lowfat yogurt
2 tablespoons mayonnaise
3 tablespoons tomato paste
1 tablespoon dry white wine
1 tablespoon fresh lemon juice
1 teaspoon Dijon mustard
½ teaspoon anchovy paste
3 tablespoons finely chopped scallion
2 tablespoons finely chopped dill pickle
2 tablespoons finely chopped sweet pickle
2 tablespoons finely chopped parsley
⅛ teaspoon black pepper
Pinch of salt

1. In a large bowl, whisk together the sour cream, yogurt and mayonnaise. Whisk in the tomato paste, wine, lemon juice, mustard and anchovy paste. Stir in the scallion, dill pickle, sweet pickle, parsley, pepper and salt. If making ahead, cover and refrigerate for up to a week.

NOTE: Nutritional values given below refer to a single tablespoon serving.

Calories 25	Protein 0 gm	Fat 2 gm	Carbohydrate 2 gm	Sodium 67 mg	Cholesterol 3 mg

ORANGE-MISO DRESSING
This delicious dressing is similar to ones served in Japanese restaurants throughout the United States. It is good atop any green salad, especially ones with peeled, seeded cucumbers. Salads dressed with this are even better sprinkled with toasted sesame seeds, ½ teaspoon per person (9 calories each).

MAKES 1¼ CUPS OR 20 SERVINGS OF 1 TABLESPOON EACH

1 cup coarsely shredded carrot
½ teaspoon grated orange zest
2 tablespoons Japanese red miso
2 tablespoons mayonnaise
⅓ cup fresh orange juice
1 tablespoon fresh ginger juice (see NOTE)
2 tablespoons rice vinegar
2 teaspoons Oriental sesame oil
1 teaspoon sugar

NOTE: Start with ¼ to ⅓ cup grated fresh ginger. Place it on a moistened double layer of cheesecloth and wring out the juice over a bowl.

1. Combine all of the ingredients in a blender or food processor and purée. Cover and chill for up to a week. Shake before using.

NOTE: Nutritional values given below refer to a single tablespoon serving.

Calories *21*   **Protein** *0 gm*   **Fat** *2 gm*   **Carbohydrate** *1 gm*   **Sodium** *71 mg*   **Cholesterol** *1 mg*

GREEN GODDESS DRESSING *Don't be put off by the dab of anchovy in this recipe; you'll never taste it, but it is needed for depth of flavor and is traditional in this classic dressing.*

*MAKES 1 CUP OR 16 SERVINGS
OF 1 TABLESPOON EACH*

½ cup plain lowfat yogurt
⅓ cup sour cream
2 tablespoons mayonnaise
¼ cup sliced scallions (including green stems)
¼ cup chopped parsley
½ teaspoon dried tarragon, crumbled
*1 teaspoon anchovy paste or minced
   anchovy fillets*
Pinch each of salt and pepper

1. Combine all of the ingredients in a blender or food processor and purée. Cover and chill for up to a week.
NOTE: Nutritional values given below refer to a single tablespoon serving.

Calories *28* **Protein** *1 gm* **Fat** *3 gm* **Carbohydrate** *1 gm* **Sodium** *35 mg* **Cholesterol** *4 mg*

ORANGE-YOGURT SALAD DRESSING *Created to enhance fruit salads, this dressing is especially good over mangoes and papayas and sprinkled with blueberries.*

*MAKES ABOUT 1 CUP OR 16
SERVINGS OF 1 TABLESPOON EACH*

1 cup plain lowfat yogurt
1 teaspoon grated orange zest
2 tablespoons sugar
2 tablespoons fresh orange juice
½ teaspoon vanilla extract

1. In a medium bowl, whisk together the yogurt, orange zest and sugar. Whisk in the orange juice and vanilla. Cover and chill for up to a week, or use right away.
NOTE: Nutritional values given below refer to a single tablespoon serving.

Calories *16* **Protein** *1 gm* **Fat** *0 gm* **Carbohydrate** *3 gm* **Sodium** *10 mg* **Cholesterol** *1 mg*

PASTA, PIES & PANCAKES

Lasagne on a diet? Yes indeed, and in four varieties. In fact, what food-lover, dieter or no, can resist the stuffed shells or linguine with white clam sauce and other pasta in these pages, not to mention generous portions of steaming shepherd's pie with mashed-potato topping or a crustless salmon quiche or individual pizzas or savory little asparagus or corn-and-pepper pancakes. No? We thought not.

LINGUINE WITH WHITE CLAM SAUCE *This is one of my favorite comfort foods. In a pinch, you might substitute two (6½-ounce) cans of baby clams and one (8-ounce) bottle of clam juice for the fresh clams called for below.*

MAKES 4 SERVINGS

2 dozen small littleneck clams in their shells
1 tablespoon olive oil
½ cup finely chopped shallots or onion
1 large garlic clove, minced or crushed through a press
½ teaspoon dried oregano, crumbled
¼ teaspoon dried red hot pepper flakes
2 teaspoons all-purpose flour
½ cup dry white wine
½ cup chopped parsley
⅓ cup freshly grated Parmesan cheese
1 teaspoon butter
½ pound linguine

1. Soak the clams in a big bowl of cold water for about 10 minutes. Scrub with a stiff brush and rinse. Put them in a large heavy pot, cover, and place over high heat. Cook until the clams open, 3 to 5 minutes. Some of the clams may be only slightly open; discard any that cannot be easily pried open. Drain the clams, reserving all of the liquid. Scoop the clams from their shells with a spoon. Measure the liquid, reserving ⅔ cup. If there isn't enough, add water to make ⅔ cup. Reserve the clams.

2. Fill a large pot with water and bring to a boil for the linguine.

3. Spoon the olive oil into a nonreactive medium saucepan and place over moderate heat. Add the shallots and sauté to soften, about 3 minutes. Stir in the garlic, oregano and hot pepper flakes; cook, stirring, for 30 seconds. Stir in the flour and cook for 10 seconds longer. Pour in the wine and reserved clam juice. Bring to a boil over moderate heat. Simmer over low heat for 5 minutes, stirring occasionally. Chop the clams and add them along with ¼ cup of the parsley and all but 4 teaspoons of the Parmesan. Stir in the butter and remove from the heat.

4. Meanwhile, drop the linguine into the boiling water, stirring constantly with a long fork until the water returns to a boil. Boil, stirring frequently, until tender but firm to the bite, according to package directions. Drain. Toss the pasta with the sauce in a large bowl (or the pot). Serve in shallow bowls, topping each portion with 1 tablespoon of the reserved parsley and 1 teaspoon of the Parmesan. Serve hot.

Calories 336   *Protein 17 gm*   *Fat 8 gm*   *Carbohydrate 50 gm*   *Sodium 166 mg*   *Cholesterol 23 mg*

MUSHROOM CANNELLONI

Although vegetarian, this satisfying dish has a rich, meaty flavor, contributed by the dried porcini mushrooms. The cannelloni wrappers are made the old-fashioned way, by pouring batter into a small skillet, as you would when making crêpes.

MAKES 4 SERVINGS OF TWO CANNELLONI EACH

CANNELLONI WRAPPERS:
- 1/2 cup milk
- 2 large whole eggs
- 1/2 cup all-purpose flour

TOMATO SAUCE:
- 1/2 ounce dried porcini mushrooms
- 1 can (16-ounce) peeled Italian tomatoes, with their juice
- 1 tablespoon tomato paste
- 1/2 teaspoon sugar
- 1 large garlic clove, minced or crushed through a press
- 1 teaspoon dried basil, crumbled
- 1/2 teaspoon dried oregano, crumbled
- 1/2 teaspoon whole fennel seeds, crushed slightly
- 1/8 teaspoon dried rosemary, crumbled
- 1/4 teaspoon salt
- Pinch of black pepper

MUSHROOM FILLING:
- 1 teaspoon butter
- 1/2 cup chopped onion
- 1 large garlic clove, minced or crushed through a press
- 1 pound fresh white or brown mushrooms, chopped
- 1 large egg white
- 2 tablespoons plain dry bread crumbs
- 4 ounces (scant 1/2 cup) whole-milk ricotta cheese
- 2 tablespoons freshly grated Parmesan cheese
- 1/4 teaspoon salt
- 1/8 teaspoon black pepper

WHITE SAUCE:
- 1 cup milk
- 2 tablespoons all-purpose flour
- 1 small garlic clove, minced or crushed through a press
- 1/8 teaspoon freshly grated nutmeg
- 1/4 teaspoon salt
- Pinch of black pepper

ASSEMBLY:
- 2 tablespoons freshly grated Parmesan cheese

1. MAKE THE CANNELLONI WRAPPERS: In a medium bowl, combine the milk and eggs with 1/4 cup cold water. Whisk until blended. Sift in the flour and whisk until smooth. Cover and refrigerate for at least 1 hour or as long as 1 day.

2. Lightly coat a 6-inch nonstick skillet with vegetable cooking spray or oil. Place over moderately high heat. (You will need 2 tablespoons of the batter for each wrapper; an 1/8-cup measure makes an ideal ladle.) When the pan is very hot, pour in 2 tablespoons of the batter; quickly tilt and turn the pan in all directions to lightly coat the bottom. The wrappers should be thin. Cook until the bottom is speckled brown and the edge is firm, 15 to 30 seconds. Turn and cook until just done, about 15 seconds longer. Transfer to a waxed paper-lined plate and top with a sheet of waxed paper. Repeat, stacking the cannelloni wrappers on the plate with waxed paper. You will need 8 wrappers. **(The wrappers can be prepared a day or two ahead, wrapped and refrigerated, or frozen for up to 3 months.)**

3. MAKE THE TOMATO SAUCE: Place the porcini in a small bowl; add ½ cup boiling water. Set aside to soak for 1 hour. Place a coarse sieve over a heavy, medium, nonreactive saucepan. Add the tomatoes and their juice. With a stiff whisk, force the tomatoes through; discard any seeds left behind in the sieve. Add the tomato paste, sugar, garlic, basil, oregano, fennel seeds, rosemary, salt and pepper to the sieved tomatoes. Strain the porcini and add the soaking liquid to the tomatoes. Reserve the porcini for the filling. Bring the tomato sauce to a boil, stirring frequently, over moderate heat. Reduce the heat and simmer, stirring once in awhile until thick and reduced to 1¼ cups, 10 to 15 minutes.

4. MAKE THE MUSHROOM FILLING: Adjust a shelf to the upper third of the oven and preheat to 400°. Finely chop the reserved porcini. Melt the butter in a heavy medium skillet over moderate heat. Add the onion and sauté until softened, 3 to 5 minutes. Add the garlic and cook for 30 seconds longer. Add the chopped fresh mushrooms and sauté, stirring frequently, until just cooked, about 3 minutes. Set aside to cool slightly. In a medium bowl, stir together the egg white and bread crumbs. Stir in the sautéed mushrooms, the porcini, the ricotta, Parmesan, salt and pepper. Set the filling aside.

5. MAKE THE WHITE SAUCE: Pour the milk into a heavy medium saucepan. Place a sieve over the pan; add the flour and lightly tap once so just a little flour sifts through. Whisk in and then tap again. Gradually whisk in all of the flour until smooth. Add the garlic, nutmeg, salt and pepper. Whisk over moderate heat until the sauce boils. Reduce the heat and simmer, whisking, for 2 minutes.

6. ASSEMBLY: Spoon about ¼ cup of the tomato sauce into a 12-by-9-inch casserole. Place 1 cannelloni wrapper, speckled side down, on a flat surface. Spread about ¼ cup of the mushroom filling in a line across the lower third of the wrapper. Loosely roll up and place, seam-side down, in the casserole. Repeat to make 8 cannelloni. Spoon the remaining tomato sauce, interspersed with the white sauce, over the top. Sprinkle with the remaining 2 tablespoons Parmesan cheese. Bake until hot and bubbly, 15 to 20 minutes. Serve hot.

NOTE: Nutritional analysis given below refers to a single serving of two cannelloni each.

Calories 349   *Protein* 19 gm   *Fat* 14 gm   *Carbohydrate* 40 gm   *Sodium* 892 mg   *Cholesterol* 172 mg

PASTA SHELLS WITH TUNA SAUCE *A good dish for hot weather, this cold pasta dish can also be made with linguine or fettuccine. It is best when made and served shortly thereafter.*

MAKES 4 SERVINGS

½ cup plain lowfat yogurt
⅓ cup sour cream
2 tablespoons dry white wine
1 tablespoon fresh lemon juice
⅓ cup sliced pitted black olives
½ cup sliced scallions (including the green stems)
½ teaspoon dried oregano, crumbled
¼ teaspoon black pepper
1 can (6½-ounce) chunk light tuna packed in water, drained
½ pound medium pasta shells (or linguine or fettucine, broken in half)

1. In a medium bowl, stir together the yogurt, sour cream, wine and lemon juice until smooth. Stir in the olives, scallions, oregano and pepper. Flake the tuna into the bowl and combine.

2. Meanwhile, bring a large pot of water to a boil. Add the pasta and, stirring constantly, bring to a boil. Cook until tender but firm to the bite; drain. Rinse under cold running water and drain again. Toss with the tuna sauce. Chill for 30 minutes. Serve cold. (If you make it further ahead of time, you will need to stir in a little more sour cream and yogurt because the pasta will absorb the sauce.)

Calories *347*   **Protein** *22 gm*   **Fat** *8 gm*   **Carbohydrate** *47 gm*   **Sodium** *262 mg*   **Cholesterol** *27 mg*

CHEESE-STUFFED SHELLS *Colorful, rich and hearty, this simple baked pasta dish can be made ahead and popped into the oven just before serving. If you can afford the calories, for a variation, add ¼ cup minced smoke lean ham (66 calories) to the cheese stuffing. Broccoli or sautéed greens make a good accompaniment.*

MAKES 5 SERVINGS

SAUCE:
> 2 teaspoons olive oil
> 1 medium (4-ounce) onion, finely chopped
> 1 medium garlic clove, minced
> ½ teaspoon dried basil, crumbled
> ¼ teaspoon dried oregano, crumbled
> 1 teaspoon sugar
> 1 can (16-ounce) whole tomatoes in tomato puree
> ½ cup dry white or red wine
> Pinch of salt

FILLING AND PASTA:
> 1½ cups lowfat small curd cottage cheese
> 1 package (7½-ounce) farmer's cheese (about 1 cup), crumbled
> 1 large egg
> 5 tablespoons freshly grated Parmesan cheese
> ¼ cup chopped parsley
> ¼ teaspoon freshly grated nutmeg
> ⅛ teaspoon black pepper
> Salt
> 20 jumbo pasta shells (5½ ounces)

1. MAKE THE SAUCE: Spoon the oil into a heavy medium saucepan. Add the onion and sauté over moderate heat un-til softened, about 3 minutes. Add the garlic and cook for 30 seconds longer. Stir in the basil, oregano, sugar and to-matoes, breaking them up with a spoon. Pour in the wine and add the salt. Bring to a boil. Reduce the heat and simmer over low heat until thickened slightly and reduced to 2 cups, 10 to 15 minutes.

2. MAKE THE FILLING AND PASTA: Adjust a shelf to the upper third of the oven and preheat to 400°. Spread ½ cup of the sauce into a 12-by-8-inch shallow baking dish.

3. In a medium bowl stir together the cottage cheese, farmer's cheese, egg, 4 tablespoons Parmesan, parsley, nutmeg, pepper and salt to taste.

4. Bring a large pot of water to a boil over high heat. Drop in the shells and stir constantly until the water returns to a boil. Stir frequently thereafter, and cook until firm-tender, 10 to 12 minutes. Drain in a colander. Spoon about 2 ta-blespoons of the cheese filling into each shell. Arrange them over the sauce in the prepared pan. Spoon the remaining 1½ cups of sauce over the tops. Bake until hot and bubbly, about 15 minutes. Sprinkle on the remaining 1 tablespoon Parmesan. Serve hot.

Calories 322   Protein 23 gm   Fat 10 gm   Carbohydrate 36 gm   Sodium 10 mg   Cholesterol 77 mg

Vegetarian Chili (page 33)

Stir-Fried Shrimp and Chinese Vegetables (page 132)

Calico Shepherd's Pie (page 83)

Sautéed Codfish Cakes (page 131)

AUNT BETTY'S COTTAGE CHEESE NOODLE BAKE

Elizabeth Stofko, my "Aunt" Betty, made this for me during a recent visit and I realized that it could be a hearty diet dish at its comforting best. A quick and easy 1950's-style casserole, it features layers of egg noodles and melting cottage cheese containing a savory beef-tomato filling reminiscent of lasagne.

MAKES 4 SERVINGS

½ pound extra-lean ground beef
1 cup finely diced celery
1 medium (4-ounce) onion, chopped
1 medium garlic clove, minced or crushed through a press
½ teaspoon dried basil, crumbled
¼ teaspoon dried oregano, crumbled
¼ teaspoon black pepper
Pinch of dried red hot pepper flakes (optional)
1 can (8-ounce) tomato sauce
Salt to taste
4 ounces fine or medium egg noodles (⅛" to ¼" wide)
1½ cups lowfat small curd cottage cheese
⅓ cup shredded Monterey Jack or mild Cheddar cheese
¼ teaspoon paprika

1. Preheat the oven to 350°. Lightly spray a 9-by-5-by-3-inch loaf pan with nonstick vegetable spray, or lightly oil.
2. Crumble the beef into a nonreactive medium skillet. Add the celery, onion and garlic and sauté for 3 to 4 minutes, just until the meat is cooked. Drain off any fat and discard. Stir in the basil, oregano, black pepper, hot pepper flakes, tomato sauce and pinch of salt. Bring to a boil over moderate heat and simmer over low heat for 2 to 3 minutes, until some of the tomato sauce is absorbed into the meat.
3. Meanwhile, bring a medium pot of water to a boil. Add the noodles, stirring constantly until the water returns to a boil; cook ⅛-inch noodles for 2 minutes (or 3 minutes for ¼-inch noodles), again stirring frequently. Drain. Toss the noodles in a large bowl with the cottage cheese and a pinch of salt.
4. Spoon half of the noodle-cottage cheese mixture into the prepared loaf pan and spread with half the meat filling. Add the rest of the noodles and top with the remaining meat. Add the shredded cheese, scattering it evenly; sprinkle with the paprika. Bake, uncovered, for about 30 minutes, until hot and bubbly. Let stand for 10 to 15 minutes. Serve hot.

Calories 348   *Protein* 28 gm   *Fat* 12 gm   *Carbohydrate* 31 gm   *Sodium* 796 mg   *Cholesterol* 73 mg

SPINACH-MUSHROOM LASAGNE *This rich and creamy lasagne is served in large satisfying squares that contain only a fraction of the calories in most versions of lasagne.*

MAKES 4 SERVINGS

1 pound fresh spinach, stemmed and rinsed, or 1 package (10-ounce) frozen chopped spinach, thawed
1 can (16-ounce) Italian peeled tomatoes, including juice
1 tablespoon tomato paste
¼ cup chopped fresh basil leaves
½ teaspoon dried oregano, crumbled
½ teaspoon salt
¼ teaspoon black pepper
6 curly-edged lasagne noodles (5 ounces)
1½ cups milk
3 tablespoons all-purpose flour
½ teaspoon freshly grated nutmeg
1 garlic clove, minced or crushed through a press
1 large shallott, minced
⅔ cup grated Parmesan cheese (2¾ ounces)
½ pound mushrooms, sliced ¼ inch thick

1. In a large nonreactive saucepan, cook the spinach in just the water clinging to its leaves, covered, over moderately high heat, stirring once or twice, until wilted but still bright green, 2 to 3 minutes. Drain and let cool to room temperature. Squeeze dry. Chop the spinach. If using frozen spinach, lightly squeeze and drain, but do not cook.

2. In a heavy medium nonreactive skillet, combine the tomatoes with their juice, tomato paste, basil, oregano, ¼ teaspoon of the salt and ⅛ teaspoon of the pepper. Cook over moderately high heat until the sauce is slightly thickened and reduced to 1¼ cups, 5 to 7 minutes.

3. Bring a large pot of lightly salted water to a boil. Add the lasagne noodles and boil, stirring gently once in awhile, until tender but still firm to the bite, about 8 minutes. Drain; hold the noodles in a bowl of cold water for up to 10 minutes. Pat dry with paper towels before you assemble the lasagne.

4. Adjust a shelf to the top third of the oven and preheat to 400°. Meanwhile, pour the milk into a heavy medium saucepan. Gently place the flour in a sieve over the pan. Gradually whisk in any flour that falls through. Tap the sieve once so just a light film of flour sifts through; whisk until blended. Repeat until all of the flour is whisked in. Stir in the nutmeg, garlic, shallot and the remaining ¼ teaspoon salt and ⅛ teaspoon pepper. Cook over moderate heat, stirring constantly, until the sauce boils and thickens. Reduce the heat and simmer, stirring, for 2 to 3 minutes. Remove from the heat and stir in half of the Parmesan and all of the spinach.

5. Spread 2 tablespoons of the tomato sauce in an 8-inch square baking pan. Trim 2 lasagne noodles to fit the pan and use the 2 trimmed pieces to complete the layer. Spread 2 tablespoons of the tomato sauce over the pasta. Add half of the creamed spinach and cover with half of the sliced mushrooms. Spread on ¼ cup of the tomato sauce and sprinkle with 2 tablespoons of the Parmesan cheese. Repeat to form a second layer. Trim the remaining 2 noodles as before and top with the remaining tomato sauce and Parmesan cheese. Bake until browned and bubbly, about 30 minutes. Let stand for about 15 minutes. Cut the lasagne into 4 squares and serve.

Calories 349   *Protein* 20 gm   *Fat* 9 gm   *Carbohydrate* 49 gm   *Sodium* 908 mg   *Cholesterol* 26 mg

RED AND GREEN ROASTED PEPPER LASAGNE
The only clue that this rich, hearty lasagne is low in calories is the calorie count itself. Layers of colorful roasted peppers and wide lasagne noodles are slathered with creamy Parmesan sauce and homemade tomato sauce.

MAKES 4 SERVINGS

1 pound (3 medium) red bell peppers
1 pound (3 medium) green bell peppers
1 teaspoon olive oil
1 medium (4-ounce) onion, chopped
2 medium garlic cloves, minced or crushed through a press
⅓ cup dry white wine
1 can (16-ounce) Italian peeled tomatoes, with their juice
2 tablespoons tomato paste
1 teaspoon dried basil, crumbled
1 teaspoon dried oregano, crumbled
½ teaspoon whole fennel seeds
½ teaspoon dried rosemary, crumbled
½ teaspoon salt
½ teaspoon black pepper
1¼ cups milk
3 tablespoons all-purpose flour
¼ teaspoon freshly grated nutmeg
½ cup freshly grated Parmesan cheese (2 ounces)
6 curly-edged lasagne noodles (5 ounces)

1. Roast the red and green bell peppers directly over a gas flame or under the broiler as close to the heat as possible, turning until charred all over. Place in a plastic bag, twisting the top to enclose, and let steam for about 5 minutes in the refrigerator. Working over a colander, peel the peppers by rubbing the skins gently under warm running water. Remove the cores and seeds; cut the peppers into 1½- to 2-inch pieces. Keep the red and green peppers separated and reserve.

2. Pour the oil into a heavy medium nonreactive saucepan. Add the onion and sauté over moderate heat until softened, 3 to 5 minutes. Add half of the garlic and cook for 30 seconds longer. Stir in the wine, tomatoes and their juice, tomato paste, basil, oregano, fennel seeds, rosemary, ¼ teaspoon of the salt and ¼ teaspoon of the pepper. Break up the tomatoes with a spoon. Bring the sauce to a boil over moderate heat, stirring frequently. Reduce the heat and simmer, stirring occasionally, until thick and reduced to 1½ cups, 20 to 30 minutes. **(The recipe may be prepared several hours ahead to this point.)**

3. Adjust a shelf to the upper third of the oven and preheat to 400°. Pour the milk into a heavy medium saucepan. Place a sieve over the pan and gently add all of the flour to the sieve but do not sift it through. Lightly tap once, so just a film of flour sifts through; whisk it into the milk and then tap again. Repeat until all of the flour has been whisked in and the mixture is smooth. Add the remaining garlic, the nutmeg and the remaining ¼ teaspoon salt and ¼ teaspoon pepper. Bring to a boil, whisking constantly, over moderate heat. Reduce the heat and simmer, stirring, for 2 to 3 minutes. Remove from the heat and stir in 6 tablespoons of the Parmesan cheese.

4. Bring a large pot of lightly salted water to a boil. Add the lasagne noodles and boil, stirring gently once in awhile, until tender but firm to the bite, about 8 minutes. Drain; hold the noodles in a bowl of cold water for up to 10 minutes. Drain and pat dry on paper towels before assembling the lasagne.

5. Spread ¼ cup of the tomato sauce in an 8-inch square baking pan. Trim 2 lasagne noodles to fit the pan and use the 2 trimmed pieces to complete the layer. Spoon ¼ cup of tomato sauce and 3 to 4 tablespoons of the Parmesan sauce over the noodles. Arrange all of the red pepper pieces over the sauce. Spread with ¼ cup more tomato sauce and 3 to 4 tablespoons of the Parmesan sauce.

6. Trim 2 more lasagne noodles as before and arrange to make another layer. Repeat the layering with the sauces, this time using the green peppers. Trim the remaining 2 noodles as before and arrange to make the top layer. Spread with the remaining tomato sauce and Parmesan sauce. Sprinkle with the remaining 2 tablespoons Parmesan. Bake, uncovered, for about 30 minutes, until browned and bubbly. Let stand for 15 minutes. Cut the lasagne into 4 equal squares and serve hot.

Calories 331   **Protein** *15 gm*   **Fat** *9 gm*   **Carbohydrate** *49 gm*   **Sodium** *794 mg*   **Cholesterol** *20 mg*

CRABMEAT-BASIL LASAGNE *Serve this luxurious seafood lasagne with steamed broccoli and lemon wedges and you can be sure no one will detect a hint of "diet" in this dish. The wide lasagne noodles are layered with fresh crabmeat and basil leaves, and spread with creamy Parmesan sauce.*

MAKES 6 SERVINGS

2 cups milk
1 bottle (8-ounce) clam juice
1/4 cup dry white wine
1 large garlic clove, minced or crushed through a press
1/2 teaspoon freshly grated nutmeg
1/8 teaspoon cayenne pepper
1 teaspoon salt
1/4 teaspoon black pepper
3/4 cup all-purpose flour
1 tablespoon powdered mustard
1/2 cup freshly grated Parmesan cheese (2 ounces)
1 pound fresh lump crabmeat, picked over
2 tablespoons fresh lemon juice
1 cup chopped fresh basil
6 curly-edged lasagne noodles (5 ounces)
1 teaspoon sweet paprika

1. Adjust a shelf to the upper third of the oven and preheat to 400°. Put a large pot of lightly salted water on to boil while you prepare the sauce.

2. In a heavy medium nonreactive saucepan, combine the milk, clam juice, wine, garlic, nutmeg, cayenne, salt and black pepper. Place a sieve over the pan and gently add all of the flour to the sieve but do not sift it through. Lightly tap once, so just a film of flour sifts through.

Whisk it into the liquid until smooth and then tap again. Repeat until all of the flour has been whisked in and the mixture is smooth.

3. Bring the sauce to a boil, whisking constantly, over moderate heat. Reduce the heat and simmer, whisking, until very thick, about 3 minutes. Remove from the heat and stir in 6 tablespoons of the Parmesan cheese. Remove 1 cup of the Parmesan sauce and reserve for the top. Stir the crabmeat, lemon juice and basil into the remaining Parmesan sauce.

4. Add the lasagne noodles to the boiling water and return to a boil. Stir carefully without tearing the noodles, cook until almost tender but still firm to the bite, about 8 minutes. Drain and rinse under cold water. Pat dry on paper towels.

5. Spread about 2 tablespoons of the sauce from the crabmeat filling in a 12-by-8-by-2-inch glass baking dish or shallow casserole. Cut 2 lasagne noodles in half crosswise and place in the dish, crosswise, to make a single layer. Spread with half of the crabmeat filling. Cut 2 more noodles as before and arrange over the crab. Spread with the remaining crabmeat filling. Top with the 2 remaining lasagne noodles, cutting them as before. Spread the reserved Parmesan sauce over the top. Sprinkle on the remaining 2 tablespoons Parmesan and the paprika. Bake until the lasagne is hot and bubbly and lightly browned, about 25 minutes. Let stand for about 15 min-

utes. Cut the lasagne into 6 equal squares. Serve hot, with steamed broccoli and lemon wedges.

Calories *326* **Protein** *27 gm* **Fat** *7 gm* **Carbohydrate** *37 gm* **Sodium** *857 mg* **Cholesterol** *94 mg*

LASAGNE BOLOGNESE *Don't compare this lasagne to ones made from dried lasagne noodles. This authentically thin version must begin with homemade pasta. A pasta machine is convenient for rolling pasta, but is not required. I have successfully used a rolling pin many times and even a wine bottle on occasion. The pasta and the Bolognese sauce should be made well ahead, even the day before, since they take a considerable amount of time to prepare. The lasagne, however, is best served shortly after removing it from the oven.*

MAKES 6 SERVINGS

PASTA:
　1½ cups all-purpose flour
　2 large eggs

CHEESE SAUCE:
　1⅔ cups milk
　¼ cup all-purpose flour
　⅛ teaspoon freshly grated nutmeg
　½ teaspoon salt
　⅛ teaspoon black pepper
　⅓ cup dry white wine
　½ cup freshly grated Parmesan cheese
　　(2 ounces)

ASSEMBLY:
　2 cups Bolognese Sauce (recipe,
　page 77)

1. MAKE THE PASTA: Put the flour in a large bowl and make a well in the center. Crack the eggs into the well. Using a fork, stir the eggs with a circular motion, gradually incorporating the flour in as you stir. Continue stirring, gradually pulling in more flour until the mixture becomes very thick. Then, using your fingers (dusted with flour), work in enough of the remaining flour to make a moderately stiff, but not dry, dough. Knead it in your hands, dipping it into the flour in the bowl if needed to prevent sticking, until smooth and satiny, about 10 minutes. Dust the dough with flour, put it in a plastic bag and let rest at room temperature for 1 hour (or chill for a day or two and let return to room temperature before rolling).

2. MAKE THE CHEESE SAUCE: Adjust an oven shelf to the top third of the oven and preheat to 450°. Pour the milk into a heavy medium saucepan. Place the flour into a sieve held over the pan but do not sift it through. Lightly tap the sieve once and then whisk in the small amount of flour that sifted through. Repeat until all of the flour has been whisked in and the mixture is smooth. Add the nutmeg, salt and pepper. Place over moderate heat and, whisking constantly, bring to a boil. Stir in the wine and simmer for 2 to 3 minutes, stirring, until thick. Remove from the heat and stir in all but 2 tablespoons of the Parmesan.

3. ROLL OUT AND COOK THE PASTA: Bring a large pot of lightly salted water to a boil over high heat (if it boils before the pasta is rolled out and cut, lower the heat, cover the pot and keep it at a simmer).

4. Shape the pasta into a 5-inch log and dust with flour. Pass it through the widest setting of a pasta machine 3 times to knead it further. Continue passing it through the machine, reducing the space between the rollers each time, until the pasta is very thin but not paper-thin (setting #3 on the electric Bialetti machine; it will vary on manual models). When the pasta become too long to handle, cut it into 4 pieces and continue. Meanwhile, increase the heat under the water to high and return to a boil. Cut the pasta into rectangles, 3- or 4-inches wide by 3- to 5-inches long; the shape and size are not important. Drop one-fourth of the pieces into the boiling water and time for 5 to 10 seconds, until they become slightly lighter in color. Do not cook longer than 10 seconds. Scoop out with a slotted spoon and transfer to a large bowl of cold water. Repeat with the remaining pieces of pasta. Remove them from the water and drain on paper towels or a clean cotton or linen towel.

5. ASSEMBLE THE LASAGNE: The Bolognese sauce should be slightly warm; if yours is chilled, heat it before assembling the lasagne. Spoon 2 tablespoons of the Bolognese sauce into a 12-by-8-inch baking pan; spread out to lightly coat the bottom. Arrange about one-fourth of the pasta in the pan (they can overlap slightly). Spoon ½ cup of the Bolognese sauce in dollops all over the pasta, interspersing it with ½ cup of the cheese sauce. Repeat the layering 3 more times. Sprinkle the top with the reserved 2 tablespoons Parmesan. Bake in the top third of the preheated oven for 15 to 20 minutes, until hot and lightly browned. Let stand for 15 minutes. Cut the lasagne into 6 rectangles and serve hot.

Calories 349   *Protein 19 gm*   *Fat 14 gm*   *Carbohydrate 38 gm*   *Sodium 696 mg*   *Cholesterol 130 mg*

MARINARA SAUCE

Authentic marinara sauce contains some anchovies—not enough to give the sauce a pronounced anchovy flavor but enough for depth and intrigue. One-half cup of this sauce will serve 3 ounces of dried pasta, such as spaghetti or fettucine. To make this into a red clam sauce you can add ½ cup clam juice (2 calories) to the tomatoes and cook it down. Then add cooked chopped clams (168 calories per cup) after the sauce has cooked (refer to page 60 for instructions on how to cook the clams, reserving the clam juice).

MAKES 6 SERVINGS OF
½ CUP EACH

1 tablespoon olive oil
2 medium (4-ounce) onions, finely chopped
1 medium garlic clove, minced or crushed through a press
3 flat anchovy fillets, coarsely chopped (1 tablespoon)
½ cup chopped parsley
2 tablespoons tomato paste
1 can (28-ounce) whole tomatoes, in their juice
Pinch of salt

1. Spoon the oil into a nonreactive medium saucepan and place over moderate heat. Add the onions and sauté to soften, 3 to 5 minutes. Add the garlic, anchovies and ¼ cup of the parsley. Cook, stirring, for 1 minute. Stir in the tomato paste and then the tomatoes and juice, breaking up the tomatoes with a spoon. Add the pinch of salt and bring to a boil. Reduce the heat and simmer until the flavors blend and the sauce thickens slightly and is reduced to 3 cups, 15 to 20 minutes. Serve hot, with freshly cooked pasta. Sprinkle the remaining ¼ cup parsley over the top.

Calories *70*   **Protein** *3 gm*   **Fat** *3 gm*   **Carbohydrate** *10 gm*   **Sodium** *357 mg*   **Cholesterol** *1 mg*

BOLOGNESE SAUCE

BOLOGNESE SAUCE *This is the rich and hearty tomato-meat sauce that is the favorite in Bologna, Italy. Here I have used more vegetables to make the battuto (seasoning blend) than are traditionally used. Some Italian chefs mince the vegetables to a paste before sautéing; however, when very finely chopped with a knife, they work equally well. When I make this sauce, I use 2 cups of it to make the Lasagne Bolognese (page 74) and the remainder to serve with pasta, such as spaghetti or fettuccine, allowing ½ cup per 3 ounces of dried pasta.*

MAKES 5 CUPS OR 10 SERVINGS OF ½ CUP EACH

1 tablespoon olive oil
1 cup finely chopped onion
1 cup finely chopped carrot
1 cup finely chopped celery
2 medium garlic cloves, minced or crushed through a press
1 pound extra-lean ground beef, such as sirloin or round
1 teaspoon salt
¼ teaspoon black pepper
1 tablespoon dried basil, crumbled
1 teaspoon dried oregano, crumbled
1 cup dry white wine
¾ cup milk
¼ teaspoon freshly grated nutmeg
¼ cup tomato paste
1 can (28-ounce) whole Italian tomatoes, with their juice

1. Spoon the oil into a large nonreactive saucepan and place over moderate heat. Add the onion, carrot and celery and sauté until softened, about 5 minutes, adding 1 or 2 tablespoons of water if the vegetables begin to stick to the pan. Add the garlic and cook for 30 seconds longer.

2. Crumble in the ground beef and cook only until half done, still slightly pink. Add the salt, pepper, basil, oregano and wine. Bring to a boil over moderately high heat and cook until the wine is completely evaporated and the meat begins sizzling rather than simmering, about 15 minutes. Pour in the milk and add the nutmeg. Lower the heat to moderate and cook, stirring occasionally, until the milk is completely evaporated, 7 to 10 minutes.

3. Stir in the tomato paste and then add the tomatoes and their juice, breaking the tomatoes up with a spoon. Bring to a boil. Reduce the heat and keep at a gentle simmer, stirring occasionally, and adding about ½ cup water each time the sauce becomes thick (about every 30 minutes). Cook for a total of 2 to 2½ hours, adding water as needed, until the sauce is thick and the meat, very tender; should yield 5 cups of sauce. Serve hot.

When reheating, it may be necessary to add a little more water or wine.

Calories 167   *Protein* 11 gm   *Fat* 10 gm   *Carbohydrate* 9 gm   *Sodium* 456 mg   *Cholesterol* 34 mg

---

S PINACH SAUCE *This simple sauce has great flavor, a beautiful jade green color and is especially good with linguine or spaghettini. Be sure to start with fresh spinach for best results and serve it right away. This recipe yields enough sauce to toss with ½ pound of dried pasta.*

MAKES 1¼ CUPS OR 5 SERVINGS OF ¼ CUP EACH

1 teaspoon olive oil
1 medium garlic clove, minced or crushed through a press
¾ cup well-drained, packed, chopped cooked spinach (see NOTE)
½ teaspoon dried basil, crumbled
¼ cup sour cream
¼ cup plain lowfat yogurt
2 tablespoons freshly grated Parmesan cheese
Salt and pepper (optional)

NOTE: Start with about 1 pound of fresh spinach; rinse well and discard just the thick tough stems. Put in a large pot with just the water that clings to the leaves after draining and shaking. Cover the pot and cook over high heat until wilted, stirring once or twice, about 3 minutes. Drain well; let cool. Squeeze gently to remove any excess liquid. Chop.

1. Combine the oil and garlic in a non-reactive small skillet and sizzle over moderate heat for about 30 seconds. Do not let the garlic brown. Add the spinach and basil and toss for 1 minute to warm and blend flavors.

2. In a food processor or blender, combine the spinach mixture with the sour cream, yogurt and Parmesan. Process to a purée. Turn out into a small bowl and stir in salt and pepper to taste. To serve, toss ¼ cup of the sauce with 2 ounces of dried pasta cooked al dente. Serve with additional Parmesan, if desired.

Calories 58   *Protein* 3 gm   *Fat* 4 gm   *Carbohydrate* 3 gm   *Sodium* 77 mg   *Cholesterol* 7 mg

---

LIGHT PESTO

When pesto, the Italian basil sauce for pasta, is made the traditional way, an enormous amount of olive oil is worked into the paste and then thickened further with pine nuts. I like the intensity of the fresh basil but prefer a lighter sauce. Here I have combined yogurt with a little sour cream (for richness), used only 1 tablespoon of olive oil and skipped the nuts. Use ¼ cup of the sauce (which will keep for a week in the refrigerator) for each 3 ounces of dried pasta. By the way, 3 ounces of dried pasta weighs 8 ounces after boiling.

MAKES 2¼ CUPS OR 9 SERVINGS OF ¼ CUP EACH

1 tablespoon olive oil
1 large garlic clove, minced or crushed
  through a press
4 cups loosely packed fresh basil
  (about 4 ounces)
1 cup plain lowfat yogurt
½ cup sour cream
½ cup freshly grated Parmesan cheese
  (2 ounces plus more for topping if
  desired)
½ teaspoon salt
¼ teaspoon black pepper

1. Combine the oil and garlic in a small heavy skillet and let sizzle over low heat for about 1 minute, until softened but not browned. Remove from the heat and let cool slightly.

2. Rinse the basil leaves and drain them well. Pat dry on paper towels. In a food processor or blender, combine the basil, garlic-oil mixture, yogurt, sour cream, Parmesan, salt and pepper; process to a purée. Toss each ¼ cup of pesto with 3 ounces dried pasta, cooked al dente. Serve at room temperature over the hot pasta.

Calories *90*   **Protein** *4 gm*   **Fat** *6 gm*   **Carbohydrate** *5 gm*   **Sodium** *248 mg*   **Cholesterol** *11 mg*

FRESH TOMATO SAUCE

You must use good fresh summer tomatoes to make this simple, delicious sauce. At other times, follow the recipe for Marinara Sauce on page 76. One-half cup of this sauce is enough for 3 ounces of dried thin spaghetti or linguine or 8 ounces of steamed sliced mushrooms (which can take the place of the pasta). The dried red hot pepper flakes are optional. Sometimes I leave them out, depending on my mood (they do, however, add a spark). One tablespoon of grated Parmesan cheese (10 calories) can be served over each portion.

MAKES 8 SERVINGS OF ½ CUP EACH

*3 pounds ripe tomatoes (6 large or
   12 medium)
1 tablespoon olive oil
4 medium (4-ounce) onions, chopped
2 large garlic cloves, minced or crushed
   through a press
1 cup dry white wine
3 tablespoons tomato paste
1 teaspoon dried basil, crumbled
½ teaspoon dried oregano, crumbled
½ bay leaf
1 teaspoon salt
¼ teaspoon black pepper
¼ teaspoon dried red hot pepper flakes
   (optional)
1 to 2 teaspoons sugar (optional)*

1. One at a time, stab each tomato onto a long fork and roast directly over a flame, turning it in the flame, until lightly blistered and lightly speckled black all over, about 1 to 2 minutes. (Alternatively, drop into a large pot of boiling water for 10 seconds and then dip briefly in cold water. Drain.) Peel the tomatoes and cut out the stem end. Cut the tomatoes in half crosswise, and lightly squeeze out the seeds. Cut the tomatoes into 1-inch chunks; you should have about 5 cups.

2. Spoon the oil into a nonreactive medium saucepan and warm over moderate heat. Add the onions and sauté until soft and translucent, 3 to 5 minutes. If they become dry or begin to stick, add 1 or 2 tablespoons of water and continue cooking. Add the garlic and cook for 30 seconds longer. Add the fresh tomatoes, wine, tomato paste, basil, oregano, bay leaf, salt, pepper and hot pepper flakes. Bring to a boil, stirring frequently, over moderate heat. Lower the heat and simmer, stirring occasionally, until thickened and reduced to 4 cups, 35 to 50 minutes. Taste to check the acidity of the tomatoes and add 1 to 2 teaspoons of sugar if desired. Serve hot, over pasta or mushrooms. This sauce improves if made a day or two ahead and stored in the refrigerator.

Calories 73   **Protein** *3 gm*   **Fat** *2 gm*   **Carbohydrate** *13 gm*   **Sodium** *340 mg*   **Cholesterol** *0 mg*

DEEP-DISH SPINACH PIE *This crustless pie has a good fresh flavor and soothing custardy consistency. You can make it ahead of time and reheat it in portions.*

MAKES 6 SERVINGS

2 tablespoons plain dry bread crumbs
2 pounds fresh spinach or 2 packages
    (10 ounce) frozen chopped spinach, thawed
4 large eggs
¾ cup milk
½ cup heavy cream
1 tablespoon all-purpose flour
¾ cup shredded sharp Cheddar cheese
    (3 ounces)
2 tablespoons fresh lemon juice
½ teaspoon dried tarragon, crumbled
¼ teaspoon freshly grated nutmeg
¼ teaspoon black pepper
Salt
½ teaspoon paprika

1. Preheat the oven to 350°. Spray an 8-inch square baking pan with vegetable spray or lightly oil. Add the bread crumbs to the pan and tilt to coat evenly.
2. If using fresh spinach, rinse well and pull off and discard any tough thick stems. Put the spinach, with just the water clinging to the leaves, into a large nonreactive pan or Dutch oven and cover tightly. Cook over high heat, stirring once or twice, just until wilted down, 2 to 3 minutes. Drain. Cool slightly. Squeeze out any excess juice and coarsely chop. You should have about 2 cups. (If starting with frozen spinach, simply thaw and squeeze dry.)
3. In a large bowl, whisk the eggs until blended. Whisk in the milk, heavy cream and flour. Stir in all but 2 tablespoons of the cheese. Stir in the lemon juice, tarragon, nutmeg, pepper, salt to taste and the chopped spinach. Turn into the prepared pan and spread evenly. Top with the reserved 2 tablespoons cheese and the paprika. Bake until puffed, set and golden brown, 45 to 50 minutes. Cool on a rack for 20 to 30 minutes. Cut into 6 rectangles. Serve hot, warm or cool.

Calories 237   *Protein 13 gm*   *Fat 17 gm*   *Carbohydrate 10 gm*   *Sodium 258 mg*   *Cholesterol 229 mg*

BEEF ENCHILADA PIE *Here is a dish with great south-of-the-border flavor that contains only a small portion of the usual calories. The corn tortillas are layered with beef, corn, green chiles and cheese to make a light but filling entrée (it's also good reheated the next day). If you can afford the extra calories, serve with Spanish Rice Timbales (page 121) for a fiesta that still comes in at about 400 calories.*

MAKES 4 SERVINGS

½ pound extra-lean ground beef
1 garlic clove, minced
½ teaspoon dried oregano
½ teaspoon ground cumin
¼ teaspoon salt
⅛ teaspoon black pepper
⅓ cup fresh, frozen or canned corn kernels
⅓ cup sliced scallions
2 tablespoons chopped cilantro (fresh coriander)
1 cup canned chicken broth or stock
1 tablespoon all-purpose flour
1 can (4-ounce) diced or chopped peeled green chiles, drained
4 to 6 corn tortillas (6-inches in diameter, 4 ounces total)
2 teaspoons vegetable oil
½ cup shredded Longhorn or other mild Cheddar cheese (2 ounces)
¼ teaspoon paprika
Sprigs of cilantro (fresh coriander), for garnish

1. Preheat the oven to 450°. Crumble the beef into a heavy medium skillet. Add the garlic, oregano, ¼ teaspoon cumin, salt and pepper. Cook, stirring, until the meat is no longer pink, about 3 minutes. Drain off any fat.

2. Reserve 2 tablespoons of the corn kernels for garnish; add the remainder to the beef and cook 1 minute. Remove from the heat and stir in the scallions and chopped cilantro.

3. Pour the stock into a small heavy saucepan. Place the flour in a sieve over the pan. Gently tap the sieve and gradually whisk the flour into the stock. Stir in the remaining ¼ teaspoon cumin. Cook over moderate heat, whisking constantly, until the sauce boils and thickens. Reduce the heat to moderately low. Add the chiles and simmer, stirring, for 2 minutes. Remove the sauce from the heat.

4. Lightly brush both sides of the tortillas with the oil. Place a heavy medium skillet or griddle, preferably nonstick, over moderate heat. Working quickly, warm the tortillas, one at a time, turning once or twice until softened, 1 to 2 minutes. Stack them on a cutting board and cut into 6 wedges each.

5. Arrange half of the tortilla wedges in an 8-inch square baking pan and top with all of the meat filling. Spoon on half of the sauce and half of the cheese. Layer the remaining tortilla wedges over the cheese; spoon on the remaining sauce and cheese. Sprinkle the top with the paprika and the reserved 2 tablespoons corn.

6. Bake until hot and lightly browned, about 20 minutes. Let stand for 5 to 10 minutes before serving. Cut into 4 squares. Garnish with the cilantro sprigs.

Calories *287*　**Protein** *18 gm*　**Fat** *16 gm*　**Carbohydrate** *19 gm*　**Sodium** *730 mg*　**Cholesterol** *49 mg*

CALICO SHEPHERD'S PIE *This Southwestern version of traditional shepherd's pie is dotted with yellow corn kernels, black olive slices and diced red pepper.*

MAKES 8 SERVINGS

1 medium (4-ounce) onion, chopped
2 teaspoons vegetable oil
2 medium garlic cloves, minced or crushed through a press
1½ cups fresh, frozen or canned corn kernels
1 medium red bell pepper, diced (1 cup)
1 pound extra-lean ground beef
¼ cup chili powder
1 tablespoon ground cumin
1 teaspoon dried oregano, crumbled
½ teaspoon hot pepper sauce
1½ teaspoons salt
½ teaspoon black pepper
2 tablespoons yellow cornmeal
2 tablespoons unsweetened cocoa powder
1 can (28-ounce) Italian peeled tomatoes, with their juice
¾ pound green beans, cut into ¾-inch lengths

¾ cup sliced pitted black olives
2 pounds baking potatoes (4 large), peeled and cut into 1-inch cubes
1 tablespoon butter
¾ cup milk
½ teaspoon freshly grated nutmeg
1 large egg
1 tablespoon sesame seeds, for garnish (optional)

1. In a large stovetop casserole or Dutch oven, cook the onion in the oil over moderate heat until softened, about 5 minutes. Add the garlic and cook for 30 seconds longer. Add the corn and red bell pepper and cook until the corn is just tender, 2 to 3 minutes. Remove to a plate and set aside.

2. Crumble the ground beef into the casserole and cook, stirring frequently over moderately high heat, until lightly

83

browned, about 5 minutes. Drain off any fat. Add the chili powder, cumin, oregano, hot sauce, 1 teaspoon of the salt, ¼ teaspoon of the black pepper, the cornmeal and cocoa. Stir to blend well. Stir in the tomatoes with their juice, breaking up the tomatoes with a spoon. Add the green beans and simmer, stirring frequently, until the sauce thickens, 10 to 15 minutes. Stir in the reserved corn-pepper mixture and the olives and simmer for 3 minutes. Turn the filling into a 13-by-9-by-2-inch baking pan. **(The recipe can be prepared to this point up to a day ahead. Cover and refrigerate. Let the dish return to room temperature before proceeding.)**

3. Preheat the oven to 375°. Drop the potatoes into a large saucepan of boiling water, partially cover and cook until soft and tender, about 15 minutes. Drain and return to the pan. Toss over moderate heat for about 10 seconds to dry; remove from the heat. Add the butter, milk, nutmeg and the remaining ½ teaspoon salt and ¼ teaspoon pepper. Beat with a hand-held electric mixer until fluffy. Beat in the egg.

4. Spread the potato topping over the meat filling, swirling decoratively. Sprinkle with the sesame seeds. Bake until golden brown, 30 to 40 minutes. Let stand for about 15 minutes before serving. Using a knife, mark into 8 large squares; scoop out with a spatula. Serve hot.

Calories 339   *Protein* 18 gm   *Fat* 15 gm   *Carbohydrate* 36 gm   *Sodium* 792 mg   *Cholesterol* 68 mg

---

BEEF TAMALE PIE *Here is a quick and easy, hearty tamale pie that's made in a skillet on top of the stove. Soft and spoonable when just cooked, it will set upon standing and can be cut into wedges for serving.*

MAKES 4 SERVINGS OF 2 WEDGES EACH

½ cup yellow cornmeal
½ cup canned chicken broth or stock
⅓ cup plain lowfat yogurt
½ teaspoon salt
½ pound extra-lean ground beef, such as round or sirloin
1 medium (4-ounce) onion, finely chopped
1 large garlic clove, minced or crushed through a press
1 tablespoon chili powder
½ teaspoon dried oregano, crumbled
½ teaspoon ground cumin
⅛ teaspoon black pepper
1 can (14½-ounce) whole tomatoes with their juice
1 cup fresh, frozen or drained canned corn kernels
½ cup sliced pitted black ripe olives
½ cup shredded medium-sharp Cheddar cheese (2 ounces)

1. In a small bowl, stir together the cornmeal, chicken broth, yogurt and ¼ teaspoon salt.
2. Crumble the beef into a nonreactive medium skillet and place over moderate heat. Add the onion and garlic. Cook, stirring frequently, until the beef is browned, 3 to 4 minutes. Drain off any fat. Stir in the chili powder, oregano, cumin, pepper and remaining ¼ teaspoon salt. Cook for 1 minute longer. Stir in the tomatoes with their juice, breaking up the tomatoes with a spoon. Add the corn. Bring to a boil. Reduce the heat so the mixture simmers. Pour two-thirds of the yogurt mixture in; stir and simmer for 3 minutes.
3. Smooth the top with a spoon. Scatter half of the olive slices over; drizzle with the remaining yogurt mixture and sprinkle with all of the cheese. Cover and simmer over very low heat, without stirring, for 15 to 20 minutes, until set. Sprinkle the remaining olives over the top. Let stand, covered, for at least 10 minutes before serving. Cut into 8 wedges and serve hot.

Calories *348* **Protein** *20 gm* **Fat** *17 gm* **Carbohydrate** *31 gm* **Sodium** *850 mg* **Cholesterol** *50 mg*

TOMATO, PEPPER AND MUSHROOM PIZZAS

Here is a great sensible recipe for delicious, nutritious pizzas. These have a crispy bottom crust, made even crispier by a light sprinkling of Parmesan on the baking sheets, and are juicy and tender within; adding sliced raw mushrooms provides moisture and flavor. Of course you can add any other toppings you like, as long as you count their calories.

MAKES SIX SERVINGS OF ONE (6-INCH) PIZZA EACH

DOUGH:
- ¾ cup warm water (105° to 115°)
- 1 teaspoon sugar
- 1 package (¼-ounce) active dry yeast
- 2½ cups all-purpose flour
- 2 teaspoons olive oil

PIZZAS:
- 2 teaspoons olive oil
- 4 tablespoons freshly grated Parmesan cheese (about 1 ounce)
- 2 medium (4-ounce) green bell peppers, quartered lengthwise
- 9 tablespoons canned tomato sauce
- 2 medium (4-ounce) plum tomatoes, thinly sliced
- 6 large mushrooms, thinly sliced (6 ounces)
- ½ teaspoon dried oregano, crumbled
- Salt and pepper
- 1½ cups shredded, whole milk mozzarella cheese (6 ounces)

1. MAKE THE DOUGH: To proof the yeast, stir together ¼ cup of the warm water and the sugar in a small bowl. Sprinkle in the yeast and let soften for a minute than stir to dissolve. Let proof until foamy and doubled, about 5 minutes. (If this does not happen, start over with fresh ingredients.)

2. Put the flour and oil in a food processor. With motor running, pour in the remaining ½ cup warm water and the proofed yeast. Process until kneaded, about 2 minutes. (Alternatively, the dough can be made and kneaded in the traditional manner.) Put the dough in a lightly oiled bowl, cover and let rise in a warm place until doubled in size, 1 to 1½ hours. Punch down, knead briefly and let rest for 5 minutes.

3. MAKE THE PIZZAS: Using 1 teaspoon of the oil, coat six 6-inch round areas on two large baking sheets. Lightly dust each of the six 6-inch areas, using a total of 1 tablespoon of the Parmesan.

4. Divide the dough into 6 equal pieces. On a lightly floured surface, pat out each piece of dough to a 6-inch round. Place on the designated areas of the prepared baking sheets. Cover loosely with plastic and let rise in a warm place until almost doubled, about 30 minutes.

5. Meanwhile, evenly space 2 shelves in the oven and preheat to 450° for 15 to 20 minutes. Remove the seeds and ribs from the bell pepper quarters and cut into ¼-inch wide strips. Spoon the remaining 1 teaspoon oil into a small heavy skillet. Add the bell pepper and sauté over moderate heat until softened, about 3 minutes, adding 1 to 2 tablespoons of water near completion of cooking to prevent drying or sticking. Set aside to cool slightly.

6. Uncover the rounds of dough. Spread each with 1 tablespoon of the tomato sauce. Cover with the tomato slices. Scatter the pepper strips over them and add the sliced mushrooms. Sprinkle with oregano and salt and pepper to taste. Divide the mozzarella evenly among the pizzas. Spoon on the remaining 3 tablespoons tomato sauce (½ tablespoon per pizza) and sprinkle with the remaining 3 tablespoons Parmesan cheese. Bake until puffed and golden brown, about 15 minutes, reversing the sheets after 10 minutes. Cut each pizza into 6 wedges. Serve hot, one pizza per person.

Calories 338   *Protein 14 gm*   *Fat 11 gm*   *Carbohydrate 45 gm*   *Sodium 461 mg*   *Cholesterol 25 mg*

CHEESE ENCHILADAS *To make enchiladas the traditional way, corn tortillas are fried in lard or vegetable oil and then dipped into chile sauce. Here they are lightly brushed with just a little oil and softened in a nonstick skillet.*

*MAKES 8 SERVINGS OF
1 ENCHILADA EACH*

*1 tablespoon plus 1 teaspoon
   vegetable oil*
*1 medium garlic clove, minced or
   crushed through a press*
2 tablespoons all-purpose flour
3 tablespoons chili powder
½ teaspoon ground cumin
½ teaspoon dried oregano, crumbled
1½ cups canned chicken broth or stock
*¾ cup shredded Longhorn or other mild
   Cheddar cheese (3 ounces)*
*¾ cup shredded Monterey Jack cheese
   (3 ounces)*
*8 fresh corn tortillas (6-inches in
   diameter)*
1 cup sliced scallions
*½ cup chopped cilantro (fresh coriander)
   (optional)*
Radish slices (optional)
Lime wedges (optional)

1. In a medium nonstick skillet, combine 1 teaspoon of the oil with the garlic; sizzle over moderate heat for 30 seconds. Add the flour, chili powder, cumin and oregano; cook, stirring, for 30 seconds. Whisk in the chicken broth. Bring to a boil, stirring constantly. Reduce the heat to low and simmer, stirring frequently, until the sauce is thickened and reduced to 1¼ cups, 3 to 5 minutes. Remove the sauce from the heat.

2. Preheat the oven to 400°. Toss the Longhorn and Monterey Jack cheeses together; reserve ½ cup for the top. Lightly brush both sides of each tortilla with the remaining 1 tablespoon oil.

3. Place a medium skillet, preferably nonstick, over moderate heat. Working quickly, warm the tortillas, one at a time, turning once or twice, until softened, 1 to 2 minutes. Then dip each into the sauce to coat both sides and place in a 13-by-9-inch baking dish. Arrange 2 tablespoons each of the cheese and scallions and 1 tablespoon of the cilantro in a line across the lower third of the tortilla. Roll up to enclose the filling. Arrange the enchiladas, seam-side down, in 2 crosswise rows as you work. Spoon any remaining sauce over the ends of the enchiladas and scatter the reserved ½ cup cheese down the center of each row. Bake until hot and bubbly, 10 to 15 minutes. If desired, garnish with the radish slices and lime wedges. Serve hot.

Calories 196   *Protein* 9 gm   *Fat* 11 gm   *Carbohydrate* 17 gm   *Sodium* 393 mg   *Cholesterol* 21 mg

ASPARAGUS PANCAKES *Fresh spring asparagus contributes its wonderful flavor and color to savory little pancakes, enhanced with just a little lemon juice. They are especially good with the Coquilles St. Jacques (page 137) or Crispy Sole Fillets (page 127) and with all of the dishes suggested as accompaniments to the Corn and Pepper Pancakes (page 90).*

MAKES 20 (2-INCH) PANCAKES

½ pound trimmed fresh asparagus, cut
*   into 1-inch lengths*
2 large eggs
¼ cup freshly grated Parmesan cheese
*   (1 ounce)*
2 teaspoons fresh lemon juice
½ teaspoon salt
⅛ teaspoon black pepper
3 tablespoons all-purpose flour
1 tablespoon melted butter

1. Bring a medium pot of lightly salted water to a boil over high heat. Add the asparagus and cook just until tender, 2 to 3 minutes. Drain and let cool to room temperature. Finely chop in a food processor or with a knife.

2. In a medium bowl, whisk the eggs until blended. Whisk in the Parmesan, lemon juice, salt and pepper. Add the asparagus and flour and stir until blended evenly.

3. Preheat a large heavy skillet or griddle over moderate heat. Brush very lightly with a little of the melted butter. Using 1 tablespoon of the batter for each pancake, spoon the batter onto the hot surface and cook until the edges become dry and dull and the underside golden brown, 1 to 2 minutes. Turn with a spatula and cook for 1 to 2 minutes longer. Transfer to a hot platter and repeat with the remaining batter and melted butter. Unused batter may be covered and stored in the refrigerator for a day or two.

NOTE: Nutritional values given below refer to a single pancake.

Calories 25   *Protein* 2 gm   *Fat* 2 gm   *Carbohydrate* 1 gm   *Sodium* 90 mg   *Cholesterol* 30 mg

CORN AND PEPPER PANCAKES *These savory little pancakes are best made fresh. The flavor of roasted red and green bell peppers, along with sharp Cheddar cheese, complements the fresh corn kernels. They are good with soups such as Creamy Mushroom (page 30) or Potato Soup with Spring Greens (page 27) and with New England Clam Chowder (page 37), Turkey with Cream Gravy (page 160) or Stuffed Eggplant (page 165). You may substitute fresh poblano chile peppers for bell peppers, if desired.*

MAKES 24 (3-INCH) PANCAKES

1 large (8-ounce) red bell pepper
1 large (8-ounce) green bell pepper
1 large egg
¾ cup milk
¾ cup all-purpose flour
½ teaspoon baking powder
¼ teaspoon ground cumin
¼ teaspoon freshly grated nutmeg
⅛ teaspoon cayenne pepper (optional)
½ teaspoon salt
⅛ teaspoon black pepper
1 cup fresh corn kernels (from 2 to 3
*   medium ears)*
½ cup shredded sharp Cheddar cheese
*   (2 ounces)*
1 tablespoon melted butter

1. Roast the peppers directly over a gas flame or under the broiler as close to the heat as possible, turning until charred all over. Place in a plastic bag, twisting the top to enclose, and let steam for about 5 minutes in the refrigerator. Working over a colander, peel the peppers by rubbing the skins under gently running water. Remove the cores, seeds and ribs; cut the peppers into ½-inch squares. You will have about 1¼ cups.

2. In a medium bowl, whisk the egg; whisk in the milk. On a sheet of waxed paper or in a bowl, stir together the flour, baking powder, cumin, nutmeg, cayenne, salt and black pepper. Add all at once to the egg-milk mixture and whisk quickly, just until smooth. Stir in the roasted pepper pieces, corn and Cheddar.

3. Preheat a large heavy skillet or griddle. Very lightly brush with a little of the melted butter. Using 2 tablespoons of the batter for each pancake, spoon it onto the hot surface. Cook for 2 to 3 minutes, until the edges become dry and dull and the bottom is golden brown. Turn with a spatula and cook for 1 to 2 minutes longer. Transfer to a hot platter. Repeat with the remaining batter and melted butter. Any unused batter can be covered and stored in the refrigerator for a day or two.

NOTE: Nutritional values given below refer to a single pancake.

Calories 46   **Protein** 2 gm   **Fat** 2 gm   **Carbohydrate** 5 gm   **Sodium** 82 mg   **Cholesterol** 16 mg

SHRIMP AND SCALLION PANCAKES WITH CHINESE BLACK BEAN SAUCE

Tender, juicy shrimp, crunchy vegetables and tasty Chinese black bean sauce turn scallion pancakes into a main course. Serve with an assortment of freshly steamed vegetables, such as broccoli florets, carrot slices and red pepper julienne, sprinkled with soy sauce and lemon juice.

MAKES 4 SERVINGS OF 3 PANCAKES EACH

1/4 to 1/3 cup shredded fresh ginger
2 whole eggs
1 egg white
1 teaspoon Oriental sesame oil
1/2 teaspoon minced garlic
1/2 teaspoon salt
1/4 teaspoon black pepper
1/2 pound shelled and deveined shrimp, cut into 1/2-inch pieces
1 cup thinly sliced scallions
1 cup fresh bean sprouts, coarsely chopped
1/2 cup finely diced celery
1/2 cup finely diced mushrooms
1 1/2 teaspoons vegetable oil

CHINESE BLACK BEAN SAUCE

1 tablespoon cornstarch
1 cup beef stock or canned broth
1 tablespoon dry sherry
1 tablespoon soy sauce
2 teaspoons rice vinegar, or 1 teaspoon distilled white vinegar
1 teaspoon sugar
1 tablespoon Chinese salted black beans
1 teaspoon Oriental sesame oil

1. Put the ginger in a double layer of cheesecloth and squeeze over a bowl to wring out 1 tablespoon ginger juice.

2. In a large bowl whisk together the whole eggs, egg white, sesame oil, garlic, salt, pepper and ginger juice. Stir in the shrimp, scallions, bean sprouts, celery and mushrooms.

3. Place a large heavy nonstick skillet over moderately high heat. Brush with 1/2 teaspoon of the vegetable oil. Using a 1/4 cup measure, (stir each time to combine the ingredients) ladle in 4 pancakes and spread out the vegetables to distribute evenly. Reduce the heat to moderate and cook until lightly browned on the bottom, 1 to 2 minutes. Turn with a spatula and cook until lightly browned on the other side, about 1 minute longer. Transfer to a warm platter and cover with aluminum foil to keep warm. Wipe the skillet with a paper towel and repeat twice, using 1/2 teaspoon oil for each batch.

4. In a small nonreactive saucepan, combine the cornstarch and broth; stir until smooth. Stir in the sherry, soy sauce, vinegar and sugar. Bring just to a boil over moderate heat, stirring constantly, until thickened and translucent, about 2 minutes.

5. Remove from the heat and stir in the black beans and sesame oil, pressing against the beans with a fork to mash them slightly.

6. Pour the warm sauce over the pancakes and serve hot.

Calories *201*   ***Protein*** *19 gm*   ***Fat*** *9 gm*   ***Carbohydrate*** *12 gm*   ***Sodium*** *907 mg*   ***Cholesterol*** *223 mg*

CRUSTLESS SALMON QUICHE *This makes an elegant lunch or brunch dish without the calories contained in a crusted quiche. It is good when served with lemon wedges and a salad of sliced cucumbers and tomatoes.*

MAKES 6 SERVINGS

*¾ pound skinless boned fresh salmon,
  cut into 1-inch cubes (see NOTE)*
3 tablespoons all-purpose flour
*½ teaspoon dried dill, or 1 tablespoon
  snipped fresh dill*
½ teaspoon salt
¼ teaspoon black pepper
4 large eggs
1 tablespoon Dijon mustard
1¼ cups milk
*½ cup thinly sliced scallions (including
  the green stems)*
2 tablespoons chopped parsley
*½ cup shredded sharp Cheddar cheese
  (2 ounces)*
¼ teaspoon paprika
1 lemon, cut into 6 wedges

NOTE: Depending on the fish and amount of trimming necessary, start with 1 to 1¼ pounds salmon steaks before trimming.

1. Bring ½ cup of water to a boil in a medium skillet. Add the salmon, reduce the heat and cover; poach until almost cooked through, about 3 minutes. Remove with a slotted spoon. Discard the poaching broth (salmon is a fatty fish so much of the fat will be in the broth). Cool slightly.

2. Preheat the oven to 350°. In a large bowl, stir together the flour, dill, salt and pepper. Whisk in the eggs, 2 at a time, and then the mustard. Gradually whisk in the milk. Stir in the scallions and parsley and all but 2 tablespoons of the cheese. Stir in the salmon.

3. Lightly spray a 9-inch glass pie pan or porcelain quiche pan with vegetable cooking spray (or lightly brush with oil). Pour in all of the filling and distribute the salmon evenly. Sprinkle the top with the paprika and the reserved 2 tablespoons cheese. Bake in the center of the oven until puffed and set, about 45 minutes. Cool for 15 minutes. Cut into 6 wedges and serve hot, with lemon wedges.

Calories 223 **Protein** *20 gm* **Fat** *12 gm* **Carbohydrate** *7 gm* **Sodium** *413 mg* **Cholesterol** *231 mg*

VEGETABLE, GRAIN & RICE DISHES

Golden-brown and bubbling zucchini par-migiana and addictively delicious potato-poblano tacos—these vegetable dishes are worlds apart, although each makes a meal unto itself. Here are dishes as homey and comforting as fried cabbage or mashed po-tatoes with gravy and as unexpectedly el-egant as wild mushrooms in a cream sauce or wild rice and pecan pilaf—a bonanza for dieters, vegetarians and all lovers of food.

ZUCCHINI PARMIGIANA *One sensible way to reduce calories is to cut back on fats. In this dish I have eliminated frying the zucchini and have not added butter to the sauce.*

MAKES 6 SERVINGS

½ pound very lean ground beef
1 medium (4-ounce) onion, chopped
1 garlic clove, minced or crushed
   through a press
1 tablespoon dried basil, crumbled
1 teaspoon dried oregano, crumbled
1 teaspoon whole fennel seeds
¼ teaspoon dried rosemary, crumbled
1 teaspoon sugar
¾ teaspoon salt
2 tablespoons tomato paste
1 can (28 ounces) peeled Italian
   tomatoes, with their juice
2 tablespoons dry white or red wine
6 medium-large (8-ounce) zucchini, cut
   lengthwise into ¼-inch slices
2 cups milk
¼ cup all-purpose flour
¼ teaspoon freshly grated nutmeg
¾ cup freshly grated Parmesan cheese
   (3 ounces)

1. Crumble the ground beef into a large nonreactive saucepan. Add the onion and garlic. Cook over moderately high heat, stirring frequently, until the meat is no longer pink and the onion is translucent, 3 to 5 minutes. Add the basil, oregano, fennel seeds, rosemary, sugar, ¼ teaspoon of salt, the tomato paste and tomatoes with their juice. Break up the tomatoes with a spoon. Stir in 2 cups of water and bring to a boil. Reduce the heat and simmer, stirring occasionally, until the sauce is thick and reduced to 3 cups, about 1½ hours. Remove from the heat and stir in the wine. **(The recipe can be prepared ahead to this point. Let cool to room temperature; cover and refrigerate for up to 5 days or freeze for up to 3 months. Reheat before using.)**

2. Bring a large pot of lightly salted water to a boil over high heat. Drop in half the zucchini slices. When the water returns to a boil, cook for 1 minute; remove with a slotted spoon. Repeat with the remaining zucchini. Lightly sprinkle the slices with salt on both sides and let drain for 20 to 30 minutes. Blot off the salt and moisture with paper towels.

3. Adjust a shelf to the top third of the oven and preheat to 450°. Pour the milk into a heavy medium saucepan. Gently place the flour into a sieve over the pan. Gradually whisk in any flour that falls through. Lightly tap the sieve once and whisk in the film of flour before tapping again. Repeat until all of the flour has been added and the mixture is smooth. Stir in the nutmeg and ½ teaspoon salt. Cook over moderate heat, whisking constantly, until the sauce boils and thickens. Simmer, whisking, for 2 to 3 minutes. Remove the white sauce from the heat.

4. Set aside 3 tablespoons of the Parmesan cheese for topping. Stir the re-mainder into the sauce until smooth.

5. Arrange the zucchini slices, overlapping them, in a large gratin or baking dish (or on 6 individual ovenproof plates). Spoon the tomato-meat sauce on top and cover with the cheese sauce. Sprinkle the reserved Parmesan over the top. Bake in the upper third of the oven for about 15 minutes, until golden brown. Serve hot.

Calories *273*   **Protein** *19 gm*   **Fat** *14 gm*   **Carbohydrate** *21 gm*   **Sodium** *555 mg*   **Cholesterol** *47 mg*

PLUM TOMATOES STUFFED WITH BROCCOLI PURÉE *These beautiful stuffed tomatoes can be served baked or unbaked. You'll have to try them both ways and decide which way you like them best. They go well with New England Clam Chowder (page 37), Deep-Dish Spinach Pie (page 81) or with Pastel de Pollo (page 158). I also love them alongside My Skinny Cheeseburgers (page 170).*

MAKES 6 SERVINGS

6 large (4-ounce) plum tomatoes
4 cups broccoli florets and/or stems,
  thinly sliced
2 tablespoons butter
1 medium garlic clove, minced or
  crushed through a press
3 tablespoons all-purpose flour
1 cup shredded Swiss or Cheddar cheese
  (4 ounces)
⅓ cup sour cream or plain lowfat yogurt
½ teaspoon salt
¼ teaspoon black pepper

1. Cut the tomatoes in half lengthwise. Using a small spoon, scoop out and discard the seeds and pulpy centers, leaving the tomato shells intact. Invert on paper towels to drain.

2. Bring a large pot of lightly salted water to a boil over high heat. Add the broccoli and when the boil resumes, cook until tender, about 5 minutes. Drain in a colander, shaking to dry.

3. If baking the stuffed tomatoes, preheat the oven to 350°.

4. Melt the butter in a small heavy skillet over moderate heat. Add the garlic and sauté for 1 minute. Add the flour and cook, stirring over low heat, for 2 minutes.

5. Combine the broccoli, cheese, sour cream, flour mixture, salt and pepper in a blender or food processor. Purée until smooth. You will have about 2 cups of purée.

6. Using a spoon or a pastry bag fitted with a star tip, spoon or pipe the purée into the tomato halves, mounding the purée. Serve at room temperature or place in a very lightly oiled baking dish just large enough to hold them and bake until tender, about 30 minutes. Serve hot.

Calories 188   *Protein* 10 gm   *Fat* 12 gm   *Carbohydrate* 13 gm   *Sodium* 304 mg   *Cholesterol* 33 mg

---

POTATO-POBLANO TACOS *The special flavor of roasted mild poblano chile peppers makes these vegetarian tacos addictively delicious. If you cannot find fresh poblanos, use bell peppers or canned roasted peeled chiles. If you make the filling several hours or a day ahead, the roasted chile flavor will permeate the potatoes.*

---

*MAKES 9 SERVINGS OF
2 TACOS EACH*

POTATO-POBLANO FILLING:

*6 large poblano chile peppers (about
   1 pound)*

3 large red potatoes (about 1½ pounds)

1 tablespoon vegetable oil

*1 medium-large (6-ounce) onion,
   chopped*

*1 large garlic clove, minced or crushed
   through a press*

½ teaspoon dried oregano, crumbled

½ teaspoon ground cumin

Salt and pepper

TACOS:

18 corn tortillas (6-inch)

2¼ cups diced tomato

2¼ cups shredded romaine lettuce

*½ cup plus 1 tablespoon chopped
   cilantro (fresh coriander) (optional)*

1 cup fresh or canned tomato sauce

*1 cup shredded mild Cheddar cheese
   (4 ounces)*

Hot taco sauce (optional)

Salt (optional)

1. MAKE THE POTATO-POBLANO FILLING: Roast the peppers directly over a gas flame or under a broiler as close to the heat as possible, turning with tongs until charred and black all over. Place them in a plastic bag, twisting the top to enclose them, and put them in the refrigerator for 10 minutes. Peel the peppers by rubbing the skins away under gently running water. Cut the peppers in half length-wise; remove and discard the seeds, ribs and stems. Tear the peppers lengthwise into strips ¼ to ½-inch wide.

2. Meanwhile, put the potatoes in a large pot and cover with cold water. Partially cover and bring to a boil over high heat. Reduce the heat to moderately high and boil until tender when pierced with a fork, 30 to 40 minutes. Drain and let cool for at least 30 minutes. (Steps 1 and 2 can be prepared hours, or even a day ahead.) Peel the potatoes; cut into ½-inch dice.

3. Spoon the vegetable oil into a large nonstick or well-seasoned skillet. Place over moderate heat. Add the onion and sauté until softened, about 3 minutes. Stir in the garlic and cook for 30 seconds longer. Add the potatoes, stirring gently once or twice. Brown, without stirring,

for 3 to 5 minutes over moderate heat. Add the poblanos, oregano, cumin and salt and pepper to taste. Cook, stirring gently once or twice, for 2 to 3 minutes longer. Keep warm.

4. PREPARE THE TACOS: If the corn tortillas are fresh and pliable, they will not need water splashed on them to soften. Heat a heavy skillet or griddle over moderate heat. One at a time, put a tortilla in the skillet. Dip your fingertips in water and fleck it on the tortilla. Turn and repeat the light sprinkling, then continue turning quickly several times until very soft and pliable. (With practice, you can heat 2 or 3 tortillas in an overlapping stack, turning the top tortilla over first then the entire stack, and repeating several times.)

5. Put a hot tortilla on a warmed plate and spoon ¼ cup of the potato filling across the center. Add 2 tablespoons each of diced tomato and shredded lettuce, ½ tablespoon of cilantro, a scant tablespoon each of tomato sauce and Cheddar, a few drops of hot taco sauce and a pinch of salt. Repeat with the remaining ingredients, folding each tortilla up over its filling. Serve 2 per portion and eat with the fingers.

Calories 300   *Protein* 11 gm   *Fat* 8 gm   *Carbohydrate* 49 gm   *Sodium* 362 mg   *Cholesterol* 13 mg

---

WILD MUSHROOMS IN CREAM SAUCE *You can use any assortment of wild mushrooms such as chanterelles, oyster mushrooms, porcini, shiitake, cremini, morels, etc. for this dish. Since they are often very expensive, you may wish to substitute domestic white button mushrooms for half the quantity specified. This is an elegant but simple dish. You might serve it with simple broiled meat, poultry or seafood or alongside a pasta with Spinach Sauce (page 78) or the Moussaka of Vegetables and Lamb (page 173).*

MAKES 5 SERVINGS OF
½ CUP EACH

1 pound wild mushrooms (see NOTE)
1 tablespoon olive oil
½ cup finely chopped shallots
¼ teaspoon dried basil, crumbled
Pinch of freshly grated nutmeg
1 tablespoon all-purpose flour
⅓ cup dry sherry
½ cup milk
1 teaspoon fresh lemon juice
Salt and pepper

NOTE: Do not rinse the mushrooms, but brush them if they are dirty. Leave small ones whole, halve medium ones and slice the large mushrooms.

1. Let the mushrooms come to room temperature if they are chilled.

2. Spoon the olive oil into a large non-stick skillet and place over moderate heat. Add the shallots and sauté until softened, 3 to 5 minutes. Add the mushrooms and cook, tossing over moderately high heat, for about 1 minute, until just beginning to brown. Add the basil, nutmeg and flour; stir to moisten the flour. Pour in the sherry and bring to a boil. Add the milk and cook until thickened, 1 to 2 minutes. Remove from the heat and stir in the lemon juice and salt and pepper to taste. Serve hot.

Calories *87* **Protein** *3 gm* **Fat** *4 gm* **Carbohydrate** *11 gm* **Sodium** *19 mg* **Cholesterol** *3 mg*

WATERCRESS OMELET *The recipe for this simple, tasty omelet is one you'll find you return to time and time again. You can top it with a dollop of plain yogurt and serve orange wedges on the side (1 tablespoon of lowfat yogurt has 9 calories, and a medium orange a total of 70 calories). Not for the cholesterol-conscious!*

MAKES 1 SERVING

1 medium bunch of watercress
2 large eggs
Pinch of salt
1 tablespoon dry white wine or milk
2 teaspoons butter
Salt and pepper

1. Bring a medium saucepan of water to a boil over high heat. Trim away 1 to 2 inches of watercress stems. Plunge the leaves into the boiling water for 1 minute (from the time it goes in). Remove, drain well, lightly squeeze and coarsely chop (you should have ½ cup for 1 omelet).
2. In a medium bowl, whisk together the eggs, salt and wine until amost blended (do not over-whisk).

3. Preheat a heavy 7-inch omelet pan over moderate heat. When very hot, add the butter and swirl until melted. Add the watercress and cook, tossing, for 1 minute. Make sure that the pan is very hot, then pour in the egg mixture. Immediately lower the heat and cook the omelet, tilting the pan or lifting the edge of the omelet so the raw egg runs underneath and cooks. Shake the pan and cook it very quickly. It will be done in 30 to 60 seconds and should not brown. Slide onto a plate, folding it over as it slides out of the pan. Serve right away, with orange wedges and a dollop of yogurt, if desired.

Calories *245*   **Protein** *16 gm*   **Fat** *19 gm*   **Carbohydrate** *4 gm*   **Sodium** *418 mg*   **Cholesterol** *569 mg*

STIR-FRIED ZUCCHINI, TOFU AND TOMATOES

This delicious tofu dish is equally good when made with asparagus instead of zucchini. If you want to make it completely vegetarian, use vegetable broth or water in place of the chicken broth and eliminate the oyster sauce (use bean sauce or extra soy sauce).

MAKES 2 SERVINGS

SAUCE:

- *1 tablespoon cornstarch*
- *¼ cup canned chicken broth or stock*
- *2 tablespoons Chinese oyster sauce*
- *2 teaspoons rice vinegar*
- *1 teaspoon reduced-sodium soy sauce*
- *½ teaspoon sugar*
- *½ teaspoon Oriental sesame oil*

STIR-FRY:

- *2 teaspoons vegetable oil*
- *2 teaspoons minced fresh ginger*
- *1 small garlic clove, minced*
- *1 medium-large (8-ounce) zucchini, cut crosswise into ¼-inch slices, or ½ pound fresh thin asparagus, cut on the diagonal into 1½-inch lengths*
- *6 medium scallions, cut on the diagonal into 1½-inch lengths*
- *2 medium (5-ounce) cakes of tofu (fresh bean curd), each cut into 12 small cubes*
- *2 medium (4-ounce) firm ripe tomatoes, cut into ¾-inch cubes*

1. MAKE THE SAUCE: In a small bowl, stir together the cornstarch and broth until smooth. Stir in the oyster sauce, vinegar, soy sauce, sugar and sesame oil. Reserve until needed.

2. MAKE THE STIR-FRY: Heat a large heavy wok (or Dutch oven) over high heat. Add the vegetable oil and tilt to coat the wok. Add the ginger and garlic and cook for 10 seconds. Add the zucchini and stir-fry for 1 to 2 minutes, to lightly brown and soften slightly. Add the scallions and stir-fry for 20 seconds. Add the tofu and stir-fry for 1 minute. Add the tomatoes and stir-fry for 30 seconds to 1 minute. Give the sauce a stir and pour it in. Cook, stirring, until thickened and boiling, 30 seconds to 1 minute. Turn out onto a serving dish and serve right away.

Calories 254   *Protein* 17 gm   *Fat* 13 gm   *Carbohydrate* 22 gm   *Sodium* 965 mg   *Cholesterol* 0 mg

GRATIN OF LEEKS *Here is delicious comfort food for a healthy diet. The leeks are light and fresh tasting, napped with a creamy, soothing sauce and Swiss cheese. If you can afford the extra calories, dot the top with a teaspoon of butter (34 calories) before baking.*

MAKES 6 SERVINGS

6 medium-large leeks, trimmed and cleaned (see NOTE)
1½ cups milk
3 tablespoons all-purpose flour
¼ teaspoon freshly grated nutmeg
½ cup shredded Swiss cheese (2 ounces)
½ teaspoon salt
½ teaspoon paprika

NOTE: Slice away a sliver of the root tip of each leek. Cut off all the dark green portions of stem leaving just the white, light green and 1½ to 2 inches of the medium-green portions. Slit the leeks in half lengthwise almost to the root end, leaving ½-inch uncut so they hold together. Soak in cool water for a few minutes; brush and rinse out any sand or dirt. Drain.

1. Bring a large pot of water to a boil. Lower the leeks into the boiling water and cook, uncovered, until tender, 10 to 12 minutes. Carefully lift out and drain.

2. Adjust an oven shelf to the top position in the oven and preheat to 400°. Lightly spray an 11½-by-7½-inch shallow baking dish with nonstick vegetable spray, or lightly oil.

3. Pour the milk into a small heavy saucepan. Place a sieve over the pan and gently add the flour to it. Gradually sift the flour into the pan, whisking as you sift. Add the nutmeg and bring to a boil, whisking constantly, over moderate heat. Simmer, stirring, for 1 minute to thicken. Reserve 3 tablespoons of the cheese for the top. Stir in the remaining cheese, along with the salt and ¼ teaspoon of the paprika.

4. Arrange the leeks in a single layer in the baking dish. Pour the sauce evenly over them and sprinkle with the reserved cheese and the remaining ¼ teaspoon paprika. Bake until hot and bubbly, about 20 minutes. Serve hot.

Calories 157 *Protein* 7 gm *Fat* 5 gm *Carbohydrate* 22 gm *Sodium* 261 mg *Cholesterol* 17 mg

PICKLED BEETS WITH RASPBERRY VINEGAR AND PEARL ONIONS

When raspberry vinegar and zinfandel wine are combined, a sophisticated, fragrant flavor and deep ruby red color are imparted to this lovely dish. The beets and onions make a good accompaniment to Turkey Slices with Cream Gravy (page 160), Crustless Salmon Quiche (page 93) or the Fillet of Sole with Mushroom Stuffing (page 126).

MAKES 6 SERVINGS OF
½ CUP EACH

1½ cups tiny pearl onions (about 6 ounces)
8 medium beets, trimmed (1 pound)
1 cup zinfandel wine
3 tablespoons sugar
1 teaspoon whole allspice, cracked
1 teaspoon coarse (kosher) salt
¼ teaspoon black pepper
¼ cup raspberry vinegar

1. Trim just a sliver from each end of the onions and peel off the skin. Peel the beets with a swivel-blade vegetable peeler and cut into ¼-inch slices.

2. In a small nonreactive saucepan, combine the wine with ¼ cup water. Stir in the sugar, allspice, salt and pepper. Add the beets and onions and bring to a boil over moderately high heat. Partially cover, reduce the heat and simmer until the beets and onions are just tender, about 15 minutes. Transfer the contents of the pan to a medium bowl and stir in the raspberry vinegar. Let cool to room temperature. Cover and refrigerate for at least 1 hour or up to 3 days before serving. Serve cold or at room temperature.

Calories *60*   **Protein** *1 gm*   **Fat** *0 gm*   **Carbohydrate** *15 gm*   **Sodium** *289 mg*   **Cholesterol** *0 mg*

FENNEL BRAISED WITH TOMATOES AND GARLIC

GARLIC *The simple, perfect flavors here need no herbs for enhancement. This recipe is a great vegetable side dish, but is also good with thin spaghetti and Parmesan cheese (2 ounces dried pasta, the usual serving size, contains 210 calories; Parmesan cheese has 10 calories per teaspoon).*

MAKES 8 SERVINGS

1 tablespoon olive oil
2 medium (4-ounce) onions, thinly sliced
3 medium garlic cloves, minced or
  crushed through a press
1 can (14½-ounce) whole tomatoes, in
  their juice
1 cup canned chicken broth or stock (use
  water for a vegetarian version)
4 medium-large (8-ounce) fennel bulbs,
  stems trimmed
Salt and pepper

1. Preheat the oven to 350°. Spoon the olive oil into a nonreactive medium saucepan and place over moderate heat. Separate the onion slices into rings and add. Sauté 3 to 5 minutes to soften, adding 1 or 2 tablespoons of water if dry. Add the garlic and cook for 1 minute longer. Stir in the tomatoes and their juice, breaking up the tomatoes with a spoon. Add the chicken broth and bring to a boil. Lower heat and keep at a simmer.

2. Trim the fennel bulbs by slicing off a sliver from the root ends. Halve lengthwise. Remove the onions from the sauce and make a bed of them in a 12-by-8-inch shallow baking dish. Arrange the fennel bulbs over them, cut-side down. Top with all of the tomato sauce. Sprinkle with salt and pepper to taste. Cover tightly with aluminum foil. Bake until tender when pierced with a fork, 45 minutes to 1 hour. Serve hot.

Calories 58   *Protein* 2 gm   *Fat* 2 gm   *Carbohydrate* 8 gm   *Sodium* 312 mg   *Cholesterol* 0 mg

GLAZED CARROTS *Instead of using gobs of butter to glaze carrots, a low-calorie version is made with chicken broth. The tang of lemon and dill complement the sweetness of the carrots.*

MAKES 4 SERVINGS

1 pound carrots, (8 medium), peeled and sliced on an angle ½-inch thick
1 teaspoon cornstarch
⅓ cup canned chicken broth or stock
1 tablespoon fresh lemon juice
1 tablespoon snipped fresh dill, or ½ teaspoon dried dill
2 teaspoons butter
Salt and pepper
1 dill sprig, for garnish

1. Place the carrots in a steamer. Cover and steam over boiling water until tender, 4 to 5 minutes.

2. In a nonreactive small saucepan, dissolve the cornstarch in the chicken broth. Stir in the lemon juice and cook over moderate heat, stirring constantly, until the sauce thickens and boils. Remove from the heat and stir in the dill, butter and salt and pepper to taste. Pour over the carrots, toss, and place in a serving bowl. Serve hot, garnished with a sprig of dill.

Calories *67*   **Protein** *1 gm*   **Fat** *2 gm*   **Carbohydrate** *11 gm*   **Sodium** *138 mg*   **Cholesterol** *5 mg*

CORN BREAD- AND TASSO-STUFFED ARTI-CHOKES

Tasso—the spicy smoked ham from New Orleans available in gourmet food shops and by mail order—flavors a moist corn bread stuffing for plump artichokes. If tasso is not available, do not hesitate to use any good smoked ham; the result will be superb. To control the calories in this dish, you must make your own corn bread in a small batch, as instructed below.

MAKES 4 SERVINGS

¼ cup coarse yellow cornmeal
¼ cup all-purpose flour
1 teaspoon sugar
1 teaspoon baking powder
Pinch of salt
1 egg white
¼ cup milk
1 teaspoon vegetable oil
4 medium (10-ounce) artichokes
½ lemon
1 teaspoon unsalted butter
⅓ cup finely chopped onion
⅓ cup finely chopped green bell pepper
⅓ cup finely chopped celery
⅓ cup minced tasso (see NOTE) or other
*   smoked ham (about 2 ounces)*
⅓ cup canned chicken broth or stock
1 teaspoon Worcestershire sauce

1. Preheat the oven to 400°. Lightly coat a 6- to 7-inch ovenproof skillet (preferably cast iron) or cake pan with nonstick vegetable spray, or oil very lightly. In a medium bowl, stir together the cornmeal, flour, sugar, baking powder and salt. In another bowl, whisk together the egg white, milk and vegetable oil. Pour the liquid all at once over the dry ingredients and stir just until blended.

2. Turn the batter into the prepared skillet. Bake until a toothpick inserted in the center comes out clean, about 15 minutes. Turn out and let cool on a rack. Crumble the corn bread and set aside.

3. Meanwhile, trim the artichokes: Cut off the stems and about 1 inch of the tops. Rub the cut surfaces with the lemon half. With scissors, snip off the prickly points on the leaves and pull off any tough outer leaves. Drop the artichokes into a large saucepan of water, add the lemon half, cover and bring to a boil. Boil, partially covered, until barely tender, about 15 minutes. Drain the artichokes upside down.

4. Melt the butter in a medium skillet over moderate heat. Add the onion, bell pepper and celery, and sauté until softened, 3 to 5 minutes. Add the ham and cook for 1 minute. Remove from the heat and stir in the crumbled corn bread, chicken broth and Worcestershire sauce.

5. Spread the leaves of each artichoke and, with a small spoon, scoop out the fuzzy chokes. Spoon about ¼ cup of the corn bread stuffing into the center of each artichoke; spoon the rest of the stuffing between the 2 outer rows of leaves. **(The recipe can be prepared**

ahead to this point. Wrap and refrigerate the stuffed artichokes. Let return to room temperature before baking.)
6. Preheat the oven to 375°. Place the artichokes in an 8-inch square baking

pan and cover with aluminum foil. Bake for 15 minutes. Remove the foil and bake until the artichokes are tender, 10 to 15 minutes longer. Serve hot or warm.

Calories 188   Protein 9 gm   Fat 4 gm   Carbohydrate 32 gm   Sodium 560 mg   Cholesterol 11 mg

ZUCCHINI "SPAGHETTI" WITH FRESH BASIL
You will need a French mandoline (expensive) or Oriental mandoline slicer (inexpensive plastic) to cut the zucchini into long strands of "spaghetti."

MAKES 4 SERVINGS

6 medium zucchini (2 pounds), ends trimmed
1 tablespoon cornstarch
⅓ cup canned chicken broth or stock
2 tablespoons dry white wine
½ teaspoon salt
⅛ teaspoon black pepper
1 tablespoon olive oil
1 medium garlic clove, minced or crushed through a press
¼ cup grated Parmesan cheese (1 ounce)
½ cup slivered fresh basil

1. Push the zucchini lengthwise through a mandoline slicer to make fine (⅛-inch) strands.

2. In a small bowl, stir together the cornstarch, chicken broth, wine, salt and pepper. Set the sauce aside.
3. Spoon the olive oil into a large heavy skillet and place over moderately high heat. Add the garlic and cook for 10 seconds. Add the zucchini strands and stir-fry for 1 to 2 minutes, until they give up some of their liquid. Stir the sauce and add it to the skillet. Bring to a boil over high heat, stirring to thicken. Remove from the heat. Stir in half of the Parmesan cheese and all of the basil. Divide among 4 shallow soup plates. Top the portions with the remaining 2 tablespoons Parmesan, dividing equally. Serve right away. If you can afford the calories, serve with sliced Italian bread to sop up the juices.

Calories 105   Protein 6 gm   Fat 6 gm   Carbohydrate 10 gm   Sodium 478 mg   Cholesterol 5 mg

QUICK KIM CHEE

QUICK KIM CHEE *Traditionally, this classic Korean spicy condiment takes 2 to 3 weeks to "pickle," but my version is ready overnight. There's no reason why it must be served with the usual Korean dishes. I like it alongside Seafood Sukiyaki (page 139), the Sea Bass, Chiu Chow Style (page 129), Thai Beef Salad (page 53), Chicken and Vegetable Yakitori (page 155) or with My Skinny Cheeseburgers (page 170).*

MAKES 20 SERVINGS OF
¼ CUP EACH

1 medium head of Napa cabbage (about 1¾ pounds)
2 medium (4-ounce) pickling cucumbers, such as Kirby
2 tablespoons plus 1 teaspoon coarse (kosher) salt
1 tablespoon grated peeled fresh ginger
2 medium garlic cloves, minced or crushed through a press
1 tablespoon sugar
1 tablespoon sweet paprika
¼ teaspoon cayenne pepper
1 to 2 tablespoons soy sauce
¼ cup rice vinegar
½ cup thinly sliced scallions

1. Discard the tough outer leaves of the cabbage. Cut the head crosswise into slices about 1½ inches thick, discarding the stalk end of the head. Quarter the slices.
2. Trim the ends from the cucumbers. Halve them lengthwise and scoop out the seeds with a small spoon; discard. Cut the cucumber halves crosswise into ¼-inch slices. Combine the cabbage and cucumber slices in a large bowl. Add 2 tablespoons of the coarse salt and toss well. Let stand for 2 hours, tossing occasionally.
3. Add enough cold water to the bowl to cover the vegetables. Drain in a colander. Repeat 2 more times to rinse the salt away.
4. In a large bowl, combine the ginger, garlic, sugar, paprika, cayenne, 1 tablespoon of the soy sauce and the remaining 1 teaspoon coarse salt. Add the vinegar and 1½ cups cold water. Add the drained Napa cabbage and cucumbers and the sliced scallions. Toss well, cover with plastic, placed directly on the surface of the vegetables, and refrigerate overnight. Taste for seasoning and add the remaining 1 tablespoon soy sauce if desired. Serve cold.

Calories 13   *Protein* 1 gm   *Fat* 0 gm   *Carbohydrate* 3 gm   *Sodium* 556 mg   *Cholesterol* 0 mg

FRIED CABBAGE

This earthy cabbage dish is heavenly. It's surprising that just a little smoked bacon can go such a long way in flavoring it. This savory side dish has a slight sweet and sour taste, with smoky undertones.

MAKES 6 SERVINGS

3 slices hickory smoked bacon (2½ ounces), cut into ½-inch squares
1 medium (4-ounce) onion, chopped
1 pound green cabbage, coarsely chopped (about 6 cups packed)
½ teaspoon salt
1 tablespoon sugar
2 tablespoons cider vinegar

1. Put the bacon in a large nonstick skillet and fry over moderate heat until crisp and golden brown, 3 to 5 minutes. Remove with a slotted spoon and drain on paper towels. Discard all but 1 tablespoon of the fat in the skillet.

2. Add the onion to the bacon fat and sauté over moderate heat until soft, 3 to 5 minutes. Add the cabbage and the salt and fry, regulating the heat from moderate to moderately low, until the cabbage is soft and golden brown, 10 to 12 minutes. Add 1 to 2 tablespoons of water any time the cabbage begins to stick or scorch. Return the bacon to the skillet, and add the sugar. Cook for 1 to 2 minutes. Remove from the heat and stir in the vinegar. Serve hot.

Calories *67*   **Protein** *2 gm*   **Fat** *4 gm*   **Carbohydrate** *8 gm*   **Sodium** *260 mg*   **Cholesterol** *4 mg*

CREAMED CABBAGE

Here is an old-fashioned vegetable side dish like one my mother used to make. I will warn you that the consistency of the white sauce is unpredictable because the water content of cabbage varies so much. If yours thins down more than you like after adding the cabbage, you can thicken it a little further by dissolving a tablespoon of cornstarch (29 calories) in 1½ tablespoons of cold water, stirring it in and cooking for 1 minute. For a variation, try adding ¼ cup finely minced smoked ham (66 calories) to the cabbage.

MAKES 6 SERVINGS

1 pound green cabbage, cut into 1-inch pieces (about 6 cups packed)
1 tablespoon butter
1 medium garlic clove, minced or crushed through a press
2 tablespoons all-purpose flour
1 cup milk
⅛ teaspoon freshly grated nutmeg
Pinch of black pepper
Salt

1. Pour 1½ quarts of water into a medium saucepan and bring to a boil over high heat. Add the cabbage and when the boil returns, cook for 3 minutes. Drain well. Return to the pan and shake over high heat for about 30 seconds to dry. Reserve.

2. Melt the butter in a small heavy saucepan over moderate heat. Add the garlic and sauté for 30 seconds. Stir in the flour to moisten and cook for a few seconds. Pour in the milk and add the nutmeg; cook, stirring constantly, over moderate heat until the sauce thickens and comes to a boil. Simmer for 1 minute. Stir in the pepper and cabbage. Add salt to taste and serve right away.

Calories *70*   **Protein** *3 gm*   **Fat** *3 gm*   **Carbohydrate** *8 gm*   **Sodium** *53 mg*   **Cholesterol** *11 mg*

MASHED POTATOES AND LOW-CALORIE GRAVY

Good and fluffy, creamy and tangy too, these mashed potatoes are fortified with yogurt or milk instead of heavy cream. You may want to serve them with the low-calorie gravy that follows.

MAKES 5 SERVINGS

4 large (8-ounce) baking potatoes, peeled and cut into ¾-inch cubes
1½ tablespoons butter
1 cup plain lowfat yogurt (or ½ cup milk and ⅛ teaspoon grated nutmeg)
Salt and pepper

1. Drop the potatoes into a medium-large saucepan of cold water. Partially cover and bring to a boil over high heat. Boil until tender when pierced with a fork, about 15 minutes. Drain and return to the pan.
2. Add the butter and yogurt (or milk and nutmeg) and beat with a hand-held electric mixer or a potato masher until fluffy. Season with salt and pepper to taste. Serve hot.

Calories 167   *Protein* 5 gm   *Fat* 4 gm   *Carbohydrate* 28 gm   *Sodium* 75 mg   *Cholesterol* 12 mg

LOW-CALORIE GRAVY

You can use beef or chicken broth or stock to make this simple gravy. One-quarter cup contains just 29 calories, so feel free to pour it over mashed or baked potatoes and meat loaf or sliced poultry or meat.

MAKES 2 CUPS OR 8 SERVINGS OF ¼ CUP EACH

2 cups cool degreased canned beef or
    chicken broth or stock (see NOTE)
1 tablespoon cornstarch
1 tablespoon butter
2 tablespoons all-purpose flour
2 tablespoons dry white wine
¼ teaspoon celery salt
⅛ teaspoon dried thyme or basil,
    crumbled

NOTE: If starting with canned broth, use one 13¾-ounce can and add water to make 2 cups.

1. In a small bowl or 2-cup liquid measure, whisk or stir together the beef broth and cornstarch until blended.

2. In a small heavy saucepan, melt the butter over moderate heat. Stir in the flour and cook, stirring, for 1 minute. Stir the broth once again and add all at once. Add the wine, celery salt and thyme. Stirring constantly, bring to a boil over moderate heat. Simmer, stirring, for 1 minute. Serve hot.

Calories 29   **Protein** *1 gm*   **Fat** *2 gm*   **Carbohydrate** *3 gm*   **Sodium** *265 mg*   **Cholesterol** *4 mg*

BROILED FRENCH FRIES *Good and crispy and golden brown but tender within, these "fries" are not fried but made under the broiler. They are good plain or with ketchup (1 tablespoon ketchup has 18 calories) or the Bleu Cheese Dressing on page 55.*

MAKES 6 SERVINGS

6 small (4-ounce) baking potatoes,
　scrubbed and cut into 8 wedges each
2 tablespoons butter
¼ cup freshly grated Parmesan cheese
　(1 ounce)
Salt and pepper

1. Preheat the broiler. Line a broiler pan with aluminum foil. Bring a large pot of water to a boil over high heat.
2. Drop the potatoes into the boiling water and partially cover the pot. When the boil returns, cook for 4 minutes; drain. Toss in a large bowl with the butter.
3. Arrange the potato wedges in a single layer on the prepared pan. Sprinkle with half of the Parmesan. Broil for 5 to 10 minutes, until deep golden brown. (The time can vary significantly from broiler to broiler so judge by color.) Turn the potatoes and sprinkle with the remaining Parmesan. Broil for 5 to 8 minutes longer, until deep golden brown. Serve hot, with salt and pepper to taste.

Calories *136*　**Protein** *4 gm*　**Fat** *5 gm*　**Carbohydrate** *19 gm*　**Sodium** *123 mg*　**Cholesterol** *14 mg*

CURRIED POTATOES WITH PEAS AND CAULIFLOWER

Here is a pleasantly spicy dish of East Indian inspiration. The sweet peas are a welcome contrast in the curried gravy. It is best made several hours or even a day ahead, so the flavors have a chance to develop. If your curry powder is already spicy-hot, you might want to omit the cayenne pepper.

MAKES 10 SERVINGS OF 1 CUP EACH

2 pounds (6 medium) waxy boiling potatoes (such as red-skinned ones)
2 tablespoons vegetable oil
2 medium (4-ounce) onions, chopped
2 tablespoons minced fresh ginger
2 medium garlic cloves, minced or crushed through a press
1 tablespoon curry powder
2 teaspoons ground cumin
2 teaspoons ground coriander
1/8 teaspoon cayenne pepper (optional)
1 can (8-ounce) tomato sauce
2 cups canned chicken broth or stock
1 teaspoon salt
4 cups small cauliflower florets (about 1 pound)
1/2 cup plain lowfat yogurt
1 package (10-ounce) frozen peas

1. Peel the potatoes and prick them all over with a skewer. Cut into 1-inch chunks (if not cooking right away, keep in a bowl of cold water and then drain and pat dry before proceeding). Spoon 1 tablespoon of the vegetable oil into a large heavy nonstick skillet or stovetop casserole and place over moderately high heat. Add the potatoes and brown very well, 10 to 12 minutes, stirring once in a while. Remove from the pan and reserve.

2. Add the remaining 1 tablespoon vegetable oil to the pan and place over moderately high heat. Add the onions and fry until deep brown in color (this is important), 12 to 15 minutes, stirring almost constantly and adding 1 to 2 tablespoons water each time the onions begin to dry out or scorch (6 to 8 tablespoons water will be needed).

3. Add the ginger and garlic and cook for 30 seconds. Stir in the curry powder, cumin, coriander and optional cayenne. Cook for 30 seconds longer. Stir in the tomato sauce, chicken broth and the salt. Return the potatoes to the pan and add the cauliflower and yogurt. Bring to a boil, stirring frequently, over moderate heat. Reduce the heat, partially cover and simmer, stirring occasionally, until the vegetables are tender, about 30 minutes. Add the peas and cook for about 5 minutes longer, just until they are heated through. Serve hot.

Calories 163   *Protein* 6 gm   *Fat* 4 gm   *Carbohydrate* 28 gm   *Sodium* 613 mg   *Cholesterol* 1 mg

MUSHROOM AND CHEDDAR-STUFFED BAKED POTATOES *These generously-mounded, double-baked stuffed potatoes make comforting diet fare. They are fat, moist and delicious.*

MAKES 4 SERVINGS

4 medium (6-ounce) baking potatoes, scrubbed
1 tablespoon butter
½ pound fresh mushrooms, finely diced
½ teaspoon dried basil, crumbled
¼ cup dry white wine
½ cup shredded sharp Cheddar cheese (2 ounces)
⅓ cup sour cream or plain lowfat yogurt
¼ cup chopped parsley
½ teaspoon salt
¼ teaspoon black pepper
Paprika

1. Preheat the oven to 400°. Using a skewer or fork, prick the potatoes 8 or 10 times and place directly on a center rack in the oven. Bake until tender when pierced with a fork, 40 to 50 minutes. Set aside to cool slightly. Leave the oven turned on.

2. Slice off a ½-inch-thick "lid" from the top of each potato. Dice the potato lids (unpeeled) and put them in a large bowl. With a small spoon, scoop out the centers of the potatoes, leaving shells about ¼-inch thick. Put the potato flesh in the bowl. Set the shells in an 8- or 9-inch square baking pan.

3. Melt the butter in a medium skillet over moderate heat. Add the mushrooms and basil and sauté just until cooked, 2 to 3 minutes. Add the wine and boil until almost completely evaporated, 1 to 2 minutes. Add the potato mixture, all but 2 tablespoons of the cheese, the sour cream or yogurt, parsley, salt and pepper. Stir together to blend.

4. Stuff each potato shell with ½ cup of the stuffing and then divide the remainder and mound it on top of each. Sprinkle with the reserved cheese; sprinkle lightly with paprika. Bake in the top third of the oven until lightly browned, 15 to 20 minutes. Serve hot.

Calories 265   Protein 9 gm   Fat 12 gm   Carbohydrate 32 gm   Sodium 417 mg   Cholesterol 31 mg

RISOTTO WITH SUMMER SQUASH AND SWEET PEAS

There are several unique characteristics and qualifications for making rice into risotto: 1. You must begin with short-grain Italian Arborio rice. 2. A large quantity of homemade unsalted chicken stock must be added slowly as you stir for about 30 minutes. 3. The grains should be separate and distinct in a creamy sauce. You must also serve it right away. Risotto is a special treat requiring wrist strength and patience.

MAKES 6 SERVINGS

1 large (8-ounce) zucchini
1 large (8-ounce) yellow crookneck squash
2 teaspoons olive oil
1 cup fresh (See Note) or frozen peas (half of a 10-ounce package)
1 tablespoon butter
1 cup Italian Arborio rice
1 quart chicken stock (page 31)
½ cup freshly grated Parmesan cheese (2 ounces)
¼ cup chopped parsley (preferably Italian flat-leaf)
1 tablespoon fresh lemon juice
Salt and pepper

NOTE: If using fresh peas, parboil them just until tender, about 3 minutes.

1. Trim the ends from the zucchini and crookneck squash; cut lengthwise in half and then crosswise into ¼-inch-thick half-rounds. Spoon the olive oil into a large nonstick skillet and place over high heat. Add the zucchini and squash and sauté, tossing or turning once in a while, until speckled brown all over, 2 to 3 minutes. Turn into a bowl and add the peas. Reserve, covered with aluminum foil, until needed.

2. Melt the butter in a heavy large saucepan over moderate heat. Add the rice and sauté, stirring until chalky looking, 2 to 3 minutes. Add about ½ cup of the chicken stock and cook, stirring constantly, until the stock is absorbed. Add ½ cup more stock (this should be approximate; if you have a ladle with ⅓-cup capacity, it will work perfectly). Continue adding stock in this manner, all the while stirring with a wooden spoon. The cooking should take 25 to 30 minutes, by which time all of the broth has been gradually added and the grains of rice are tender but firm to the bite (when done there will be no broth, but grains in a thick creamy sauce). Do not rush as the full cooking time will be needed to turn out a perfect risotto. Add the reserved vegetables to the pan and stir over moderate heat until they are heated through, about 3 minutes. Remove from the heat and stir in the Parmesan, parsley and lemon juice. Add salt and pepper to taste. Serve right away.

Calories 265   Protein 9 gm   Fat 7 gm   Carbohydrate 41 gm   Sodium 178 mg   Cholesterol 12 mg

THREE-GRAIN PILAF WITH MUSHROOMS *If you have not yet discovered the special toasted nutty flavor of kasha (roasted buckwheat groats), try this. It's healthy and very delicious. If you are a kasha fan already, dig in.*

MAKES 10 SERVINGS OF
SLIGHTLY UNDER 1 CUP EACH

½ cup whole barley
1 cup boiling water
2 teaspoons butter
½ pound fresh mushrooms, sliced
1 large egg
¾ cup kasha (roasted buckwheat groats)
1 tablespoon vegetable oil
¾ cup long-grain white rice
2 medium (4-ounce) onions, chopped
1 large garlic clove, minced or crushed
   through a press
3 cups canned beef broth or stock
¼ cup chopped parsley
Salt and pepper

1. Put the barley in a small bowl and pour the boiling water over it. Let soak for 1 to 1½ hours; drain.
2. Melt the butter in a heavy medium saucepan over moderately high heat. Add the mushrooms and sauté, tossing, until browned. If the pan seems too dry, add a tablespoon of water to encourage the cooking. The mushrooms will be dry at first and then release their juices. Transfer to a plate and reserve.
3. In a small bowl, stir the egg with a fork. Stir in the kasha and then dump into the pan you just used. Stir constantly over moderately high heat until dry and lightly toasted, 2 to 3 minutes. Turn out onto a plate and reserve.
4. Spoon the vegetable oil into the same saucepan and stir in the white rice. Stirring constantly, cook over moderate heat until golden, 2 to 3 minutes. Add the onions and cook, stirring, to soften, about 3 minutes. Add the garlic and cook for 30 seconds longer. Add the drained barley, kasha and mushrooms to the pan. Add the beef broth and bring to a boil, stirring, over high heat. Reduce the heat to low, cover tightly and simmer, stirring gently once or twice, until the grains are tender and the liquid is absorbed, about 15 minutes. Fluff with a fork. Stir in the parsley, and season with salt and pepper to taste. Serve hot. The pilaf will remain hot in a covered pot for half an hour or so.

Calories *186*   **Protein** *6 gm*   **Fat** *4 gm*   **Carbohydrate** *34 gm*   **Sodium** *266 mg*   **Cholesterol** *30 mg*

FRAGRANT BASMATI RICE TIMBALES *Basmati rice, with its special nutty flavor, is the most elegant of rices. Serve these portion-controlled timbales with Indian dishes. They are especially good with the Aromatic Chicken Curry on page 151.*

MAKES 4 SERVINGS

½ cup basmati rice
4 cardamom pods
4 whole cloves
1 cinnamon stick (3-inch)
1 teaspoon grated fresh ginger
¼ teaspoon salt

1. Place the rice in a medium bowl and fill with cold water; pour off the water. Repeat 3 or 4 times, to rinse the rice, until the water remains clear. Drain the rice in a sieve. Place in a small heavy saucepan and add 1 cup cold water. Add the cardamom pods, cloves, cinnamon, ginger and salt. Let the rice soak for 30 minutes.
2. Place the pan over high heat and bring to a boil. Reduce the heat to low, cover and simmer until the water is absorbed, about 12 minutes. Remove from the heat and let stand, tightly covered, for at least 15 minutes. (The rice will hold for at least 30 minutes.)
3. To serve, fluff the rice with a fork. Pack a scant ½ cup into a ½-cup measure. Invert onto a plate; repeat 3 more times.

Calories 86   *Protein* 2 gm   *Fat* 0 gm   *Carbohydrate* 19 gm   *Sodium* 137 mg   *Cholesterol* 0 mg

SPINACH RICE WITH TOMATOES

This is a simple and tasty dish flavored with a little fresh or dried dill. It can be prepared hours ahead of time and can be made with frozen spinach if you don't want to bother with fresh. It is especially good with the Broiled Feta Chicken on page 157 or the Fillet of Sole with Mushroom Stuffing on page 126. Of course, it is equally delicious alongside simple broiled seafood dishes.

MAKES 6 SERVINGS

1 tablespoon vegetable oil
1 cup long-grain white rice
1 medium (4-ounce) onion, chopped
1 medium garlic clove, minced or
 crushed through a press
1 can (14½-ounce) whole tomatoes,
 in their juice
1 tablespoon minced fresh dill or
 ½ teaspoon dried dill
2 cups cooked well-drained chopped
 spinach (see NOTE)
1 tablespoon fresh lemon juice
Salt and pepper

NOTE: If using fresh spinach, start with 2 pounds and follow the cooking instructions on page 70; if using frozen, start with 2 packages (10 ounces each), thawed, with excess liquid squeezed out to yield 2 cups.

1. Spoon the vegetable oil into a non-reactive medium saucepan. Add the rice and stir over moderate heat until toasted golden brown all over, 3 to 5 minutes. Add the onion and garlic and stir over moderate heat to soften, about 3 minutes. Add the tomatoes with their juice, breaking up the tomatoes with a spoon. Stir in the dill, spinach, lemon juice and ½ cup water. Bring to a simmer, stirring frequently, over moderate heat. Cover tightly and cook over very low heat until the liquid is absorbed (there isn't much liquid because most of it is contained in the spinach and tomatoes), stirring gently once or twice, about 20 minutes. Remove from the heat; let stand for 10 minutes. Sprinkle lightly with salt and pepper to taste. Fluff with a fork and serve hot.

Calories 168 *Protein* 5 gm *Fat* 3 gm *Carbohydrate* 32 gm *Sodium* 156 mg *Cholesterol* 0 mg

SPANISH RICE TIMBALES *This simple version of Spanish rice fits nicely into a controlled calorie-count diet and goes especially well with the Beef Enchilada Pie on page 82 or the Red and Yellow Stuffed Peppers on page 163.*

MAKES 4 SERVINGS

1 teaspoon vegetable oil
½ cup long-grain white rice
½ cup chopped onion
1 large garlic clove, minced or crushed
  through a press
½ cup diced tomato
1 cup canned chicken broth or stock
½ teaspoon chile powder
¼ teaspoon dried oregano, crumbled
¼ teaspoon salt
Pinch of black pepper

1. In a small nonreactive saucepan, cook the oil and rice over moderately high heat, stirring constantly, until the rice is golden, 3 to 4 minutes.

2. Add the onion and garlic and sauté, stirring constantly, for 1 minute. Add the tomato and cook until heated through, about 1 minute. Add the broth, chile powder, oregano, salt and pepper and bring to a boil. Reduce the heat to moderately low, cover tightly and simmer until the rice is tender and the liquid is absorbed, about 15 minutes.

3. Fluff the rice with a fork and let stand, covered, for 10 to 15 minutes before serving. **(The rice can be made up to 3 hours ahead. Set aside at room temperature. Reheat gently over low heat.)**

4. For each timbale, pack ¼ of the rice into a ½-cup measure or timbale mold and turn out onto a dinner plate.

Calories *116*   **Protein** *3 gm*   **Fat** *2 gm*   **Carbohydrate** *22 gm*   **Sodium** *393 mg*   **Cholesterol** *0 mg*

WILD RICE AND PECAN PILAF *All-American wild rice is combined with brown rice and toasted pecans to create a good and grainy pilaf accented with fresh mushrooms and herbs.*

MAKES 6 SERVINGS

½ cup wild rice
¼ cup chopped pecans (1 ounce)
1 tablespoon vegetable oil
⅔ cup brown rice
2 medium (4-ounce) onions, chopped
1 medium garlic clove, minced or
* crushed through a press*
½ pound fresh mushrooms, sliced
½ teaspoon dried oregano, crumbled
½ teaspoon ground cumin
2 cups canned chicken broth or stock

1. Rinse the wild rice by placing it in a medium bowl; fill with water and carefully pour off the water so the clean grains stay behind in the bowl. Repeat 2 or 3 times. Cover with warm tap water by 1 inch and let soak for 1 hour. Drain.
2. Put the pecans in a small dry skillet and toast over moderate heat, shaking the pan, until lightly browned, about 2 minutes. Turn out and reserve.
3. Spoon the vegetable oil into a heavy medium saucepan and add the brown rice. Stir over moderate heat until toasted and lightly browned, 2 to 3 minutes. Add the chopped onions and sauté to soften, about 3 minutes. Add the garlic and cook for 30 seconds longer. Stir in the mushrooms, oregano and cumin; cook, stirring frequently, for 2 to 3 minutes. Pour in the chicken broth and bring to a boil. Add the wild rice, cover tightly and simmer over low heat, stirring gently once or twice, until the grains are tender and the broth is absorbed, about 45 minutes. During the last 5 minutes, uncover and let the moisture evaporate. Fluff and turn out onto a platter. Top with the toasted pecans and serve hot.

Calories 208   *Protein* 6 gm   *Fat* 7 gm   *Carbohydrate* 32 gm   *Sodium* 340 mg   *Cholesterol* 0 mg

LEMON-DILL RICE *Here is a lovely, light and refreshing rice dish that is simple to prepare. It is good with meat or seafood and many vegetable dishes.*

MAKES 8 SERVINGS

1 tablespoon olive oil
1 cup long-grain white rice
1 cup finely diced celery
1 medium (4-ounce) onion, chopped
1 medium garlic clove, minced or
    crushed through a press
1¾ cups canned chicken broth or stock
2 tablespoons fresh lemon juice
1 tablespoon butter
3 tablespoons minced fresh dill
2 teaspoons sugar
¼ teaspoon black pepper
Pinch of salt, or to taste
4 lemon slices
1 sprig of dill, for garnish

1. Spoon the olive oil into a nonreactive medium saucepan and stir in the rice. Cook over moderate heat, stirring, until the grains are golden brown, 3 to 5 minutes.

2. Add the celery, onion and garlic and stir over moderate heat until softened, about 3 minutes. Stir in the chicken broth, lemon juice, butter, minced dill, sugar, pepper and salt. Bring to a boil. Float the lemon slices on top, cover and simmer over low heat until the rice is tender and the liquid is absorbed, 15 to 18 minutes. Let stand for 10 minutes. Serve hot, garnished with a fresh dill sprig.

Calories 132   **Protein** 2 gm   **Fat** 4 gm   **Carbohydrate** 22 gm   **Sodium** 266 mg   **Cholesterol** 4 mg

---

CHAPTER SIX

SEAFOOD, POULTRY & MEAT ENTREES

The mainstay of dinnertime, whether it's a family or company affair, includes foods you'd never expect to find at 350 calories or fewer per (hearty) portion. Coquilles St. Jacques, e.g., old-fashioned sautéed codfish cakes, meat loaf or cheeseburgers on toasted buns. For notable occasions, a festive chicken jambalaya or seafood sukiyaki—even an authentic moussaka with lamb, potatoes and eggplant.

FILLET OF SOLE WITH MUSHROOM STUFFING

Just about everyone loves low-calorie fillets of sole—especially when they are filled with mushroom stuffing. The recipe is simple to put together and even simpler if you grind the mushrooms in a food processor. A green vegetable or Glazed Carrots (page 106) make a good accompaniment.

MAKES 4 SERVINGS

STUFFING:

1 tablespoon olive oil
1 medium (4-ounce) onion, finely chopped
¾ pound fresh mushrooms, coarsely ground in a food processor or finely chopped with a knife
¼ cup dry white wine
¼ teaspoon dried thyme, crumbled
¼ cup plain dry bread crumbs
¼ cup chopped parsley
1 tablespoon fresh lemon juice
Pinch of black pepper
Salt to taste

SOLE:

8 small (4-ounce) fillets of sole (thawed if frozen)
2 teaspoons melted butter
1 tablespoon plain dry bread crumbs
¼ teaspoon paprika
1 lemon, cut into wedges
4 small parsley sprigs, for garnish

1. MAKE THE STUFFING: Adjust a shelf to the top third of the oven and preheat to 375°. Spoon the olive oil into a nonreactive large skillet and place over moderate heat. Add the onion and sauté to soften and lightly color, about 3 minutes. Add the mushrooms and cook, stirring, over moderately high heat for 2 minutes, until they release their juices. Pour in the wine and thyme and cook until the wine is completely evaporated, 2 to 3 minutes. Turn into a medium bowl and let cool slightly.

2. Stir in the bread crumbs, parsley, lemon juice, pepper and a pinch of salt to taste.

3. PREPARE THE SOLE: Spoon 2 tablespoons of water into a 13-by-9-inch shallow glass baking dish. Put in 4 of the fillets, flattest side up (three will run lengthwise and one, crosswise). Spread each with one-fourth of the mushroom stuffing (about ⅓ cup each). Top with 4 fillets, flattest sides down. Brush the tops with the melted butter. Sprinkle on the bread crumbs and paprika. Bake until just cooked through (the fish will easily flake and be opaque throughout), about 15 minutes. With a long spatula, transfer to hot dinner plates. Garnish the plates with lemon wedges and parsley sprigs. Serve hot.

Calories 324   **Protein** *46 gm*   **Fat** *9 gm*   **Carbohydrate** *15 gm*   **Sodium** *268 mg*   **Cholesterol** *114 mg*

CRISPY SOLE FILLETS

This is a simple but delicious way to fry coated sole fillets with just 1 teaspoon of oil per serving. The secret to their crispiness is in adding grated Parmesan cheese to the cornmeal coating. For a simple dinner you might serve Broiled French Fries (page 114) or Zappy Cole Slaw (page 40) and Glazed Carrots (page 106) alongside. For a more elegant dinner, start with Oysters au Gratin (page 142) or New England Clam Chowder (page 37) and then serve the Asparagus Pancakes (page 85) on the plate with the crispy sole.

MAKES 4 SERVINGS

*4 medium (6-ounce) sole fillets
   (thawed if frozen)
3 tablespoons all-purpose flour
1 large egg
¼ cup yellow cornmeal
¼ cup freshly grated Parmesan cheese
   (1 ounce)
½ teaspoon dried basil, crumbled
¼ teaspoon dried thyme, crumbled
½ teaspoon salt
⅛ teaspoon black pepper
4 teaspoons vegetable oil
Lemon wedges, for garnish*

1. Put the fillets on a double layer of paper towels to absorb some of the moisture.
2. Spoon the flour onto a dinner plate or sheet of waxed paper. With a fork, beat the egg with 2 teaspoons of water in a pie pan until blended. On a sheet of waxed paper or on a dinner plate, combine the cornmeal, Parmesan, basil, thyme, salt and pepper.
3. Dredge one fillet in the flour to coat both sides lightly. Dip it next in the egg mixture, then in the cornmeal mixture, turning it once to coat both sides lightly. Place on a sheet of waxed paper. Repeat with the remaining fillets.
4. Place a large heavy skillet over moderately high heat. When the pan is hot, coat with 2 teaspoons of the vegetable oil. Place two coated fillets in the pan and brown well on the first side, about 2 minutes, until golden brown. Turn with a spatula and cook the other side about 1 minute longer, just until opaque and flaky throughout. Transfer to hot dinner plates and repeat with the remaining oil and fillets. Serve hot with wedges of lemon.

Calories *296*   **Protein** *37 gm*   **Fat** *10 gm*   **Carbohydrate** *12 gm*   **Sodium** *542 mg*   **Cholesterol** *155 mg*

FLOUNDER FILLETS WITH TOMATO-ORANGE SAUCE

These flour- and cornmeal-coated flounder or sole fillets are pan-fried in almost no oil and served with a simple fresh orange and tomato sauce. If fresh flounder fillets are not available, frozen ones can be used (thaw and pat dry first).

MAKES 4 SERVINGS

SAUCE:

¾ cup fresh orange juice
¼ cup finely chopped shallots or onion
2 medium (4-ounce) tomatoes
1 tablespoon fresh lemon juice
1 tablespoon butter
2 tablespoons chopped parsley
Pinch each of salt and pepper

FISH FILLETS:

¼ cup all-purpose flour
3 tablespoons yellow cornmeal
8 small flounder or sole fillets (1¼ pounds total weight)
4 teaspoons vegetable oil
Lemon wedges and parsley sprigs, for garnish

1. **MAKE THE SAUCE:** Combine the orange juice and shallots in a small nonreactive saucepan and boil over moderate heat until reduced by half, 5 to 7 minutes. Remove from the heat.

2. Peel the tomatoes: if you have a gas flame, jab a tomato onto a long fork and turn directly in the flame for 30 seconds to 1 minute, until blistered all over. Repeat with the second tomato. Alternatively, dip the tomatoes into boiling water for 10 to 15 seconds. Peel the tomatoes. Cut them in half crosswise and gently squeeze out the seeds. Chop the tomatoes into ½-inch dice; add the reduced orange juice mixture. Place over moderate heat and bring to a boil. Reduce the heat and simmer for 2 to 3 minutes to blend the flavors. Remove from the heat and stir in the lemon juice and butter until the butter is blended into the sauce. Stir in the chopped parsley and salt and pepper.

3. **PREPARE THE FISH FILLETS:** In a shallow dish or pie pan, stir together the flour and cornmeal. One at a time, dredge the fish fillets in the mixture, lightly coating both sides.

4. Place a large nonstick or well-seasoned skillet over moderate heat. When hot, spoon in 2 teaspoons of the vegetable oil. Add half of the fish fillets in a single layer without crowding and brown

well over moderately high heat, about 2 minutes. Lower the heat and turn the fillets. Cook just until done (the fish will flake easily), about 1 minute longer. Put on a hot platter and repeat with the remaining 2 teaspoons oil and the remaining 4 fillets.

5. To serve, place 2 fillets on each plate and spoon about ¼ cup of the tomato-orange sauce over. Serve hot, with lemon wedges and parsley sprigs.

Calories 287   **Protein** 29 gm   **Fat** 9 gm   **Carbohydrate** 20 gm   **Sodium** 184 mg   **Cholesterol** 76 mg

---

SEA BASS, CHIU CHOW STYLE *Chiu Chow is the last great regional Chinese cuisine America has yet to discover. Although this cooking includes many important and delicious dishes, it is famous in particular for fish and seafood and for rich stocks and broths. In this notable example, an aromatic fish stock is flavored with ginger and cilantro for poaching the whole fish. The broth is then ladled over more cilantro to make it even tastier and more fragrant. By the way, the Chinese never flip over a fish after taking the meat from one side, believing this will cause a fishing boat to turn over in the water.*

MAKES 4 SERVINGS

1½ quarts Fragrant Fish Stock (halve the recipe on the next page)
2 tablespoons fresh ginger julienne
2 tablespoons reduced-sodium soy sauce
2 medium (1½ pounds each cleaned weight) whole, fresh black sea bass or striped sea bass or red snapper, flounder or sea trout
1 medium-large bunch of cilantro (fresh coriander), coarse stems removed
1 medium-small bunch of flat-leaf parsley, coarse stems removed
1 small red or green fresh hot chile pepper, such as jalapeño, quartered lengthwise, seeded and slivered

1. In a large wok, Dutch oven or fish poacher, combine the fish stock, ginger and soy sauce. Bring to a boil over moderate heat. Reduce the heat to low.
2. Tear off 4 sheets of aluminum foil, each measuring about 12-by-16 inches. Fold them lengthwise into thirds to make strips 4-by-16 inches. Place 2 strips under each bass and lower the fish into the stock (depending on your pot you may have to poach them in 2 batches). Return the stock to a boil over moderate heat. Reduce the heat, cover and poach until a chopstick easily pierces the flesh at the thickest part, 10 to 12 minutes. Remove the fish on the foil to a large deep platter. Pull out the foil and discard.

3. Scatter the cilantro, flat-leaf parsley and chile pepper over the fish. Ladle the hot broth over all to cook them.

4. To serve, use 2 large spoons to lift off the flesh from the top side of each bass and put the portions into shallow soup plates. Spoon on some of the parsley, ginger, chile and broth and serve hot. Starting at the head of each fish left in the broth, pull up the skeleton and discard. The rest of the fish will remain warm in the broth.

Calories 264 **Protein** *44 gm* **Fat** *5 gm* **Carbohydrate** *10 gm* **Sodium** *637 mg* **Cholesterol** *100 mg*

FRAGRANT FISH STOCK *To my mind it is most practical to make 3 quarts of this stock and freeze half. You need only half of the recipe for the Sea Bass, Chiu Chow Style. If you don't want to do that, simply halve this recipe and make exactly what you will use in one day.*

MAKES 3 QUARTS: 12 SERVINGS OF 1 CUP EACH

3 pounds fish bones and heads from non-oily fish such as sea bass, halibut, haddock, sole, flounder, etc.
1 large (8-ounce) onion, sliced
1 large garlic clove, sliced
5 slices of fresh ginger, each the size of a quarter
1/2 cup Chinese rice wine or dry sherry
3 large parsley sprigs
3 large cilantro (fresh coriander) sprigs

1. In a large heavy stockpot or Dutch oven, combine all of the ingredients with 3 quarts of cold water. Bring to a boil, stirring occasionally, over moderate heat. Lower the heat and simmer, uncovered, for 30 minutes, skimming any foam that rises to the surface and stirring once in a while. Strain through a colander and discard the solids. Strain again, through dampened cheesecloth or a fine sieve. If not using the same day, let cool to room temperature. Cover and refrigerate for 1 day or freeze for up to several months.

Calories 30 **Protein** *3 gm* **Fat** *0 gm* **Carbohydrate** *4 gm* **Sodium** *121 mg* **Cholesterol** *11 mg*

SAUTEED CODFISH CAKES *Golden, crisp fried fish cakes on a diet? Yes, when you follow this streamlined recipe. The cod cakes are hearty and satisfying, especially when accompanied with the Zappy Cole Slaw on page 40.*

MAKES 4 SERVINGS OF
3 CAKES EACH

1 pound fresh cod fillets, skinned
1 large (8 ounce) baking potato, peeled
* and cut into 1-inch chunks*
1 whole egg
1 egg white
¼ cup milk
1 tablespoon fresh lemon juice
3 teaspoons vegetable oil
1 medium (4-ounce) onion, finely chopped
1 garlic clove, minced or crushed
* through a press*
3 tablespoons minced fresh dill
½ teaspoon salt
¼ teaspoon black pepper
½ teaspoon grated lemon zest
1 teaspoon Worcestershire sauce
¼ teaspoon Tabasco or hot pepper sauce
½ cup thinly sliced scallions
¾ cup finely crushed unsalted soda crackers
2 teaspoons unsalted butter
4 teaspoons chopped fresh parsley
4 lemon wedges, for garnish

1. Place the cod fillets on a plate in a steamer and steam, covered, over moderate heat until opaque throughout and the edges flake easily with a fork, 6 to 8 minutes. Let cool. Flake the fish into small pieces.
2. Put the potato chunks in a small saucepan and cover with cold water. Bring to a boil, partially covered, over moderately high heat. Cook until tender, 10 to 12 minutes; drain well. Transfer to a medium bowl and mash with a fork until smooth. Stir in the whole egg, egg white, milk and lemon juice.
3. In a small skillet, preferably nonstick, heat 1 teaspoon of the oil. Add the onion and sauté over moderate heat until softened, 3 to 5 minutes. Add the garlic and cook for 1 minute longer. Remove from the heat and let cool slightly.
4. Stir the sautéed onion, dill, salt, pepper, lemon zest, Worcestershire, Tabasco, scallions, flaked cod and half of the cracker crumbs into the potato mixture; blend well. Cover and refrigerate until firm, about 1 hour. **(The codfish mixture can be prepared up to 1 day in advance.)**
5. Place 3 tablespoons of the remaining cracker crumbs on a sheet of waxed paper. Divide the fish mixture in half. Using a ¼-cup measure, scoop out 6 codfish cakes and drop them onto the cracker crumbs; turn to coat both sides with the crumbs as you shape the mixture into 2½-inch cakes. Repeat with the remaining 3 tablespoons crumbs and cod mixture to make 6 more fish cakes.
6. In a large heavy skillet, melt 1 teaspoon of the butter in 1 teaspoon of the remaining vegetable oil over moderately high heat. Add half of the codfish cakes, reduce the heat to moderate and fry until crusty and golden brown on the bot-

tom, 8 to 10 minutes. Turn and cook until golden on the second side, about 5 minutes longer. Repeat with the remaining 1 teaspoon oil, 1 teaspoon butter and

6 codfish cakes. Serve 3 fish cakes per person. Sprinkle each serving with 1 teaspoon of the parsley and serve with a lemon wedge.

Calories 298 *Protein* 27 gm *Fat* 10 gm *Carbohydrate* 25 gm *Sodium* 412 mg *Cholesterol* 125 mg

STIR-FRIED SHRIMP AND CHINESE VEGETABLES *Because the vegetables are briefly blanched first, this streamlined stir-frying technique requires a minimum of oil—just 1 tablespoon. Each serving measures a generous 2 cups.*

MAKES 4 SERVINGS

½ pound fresh snow peas, trimmed
2 large celery ribs, cut into ½-inch dice
½ pound (4 cups) broccoli florets
¾ cup canned chicken broth or stock
1 tablespoon cornstarch
2 tablespoons dry sherry
2 tablespoons soy sauce
1 teaspoon sugar
1 tablespoon vegetable oil
3 tablespoons minced fresh ginger
1 tablespoon minced fresh hot green chile pepper, such as jalapeño, with seeds
1 garlic clove, minced or crushed through a press
1½ pounds medium shrimp, shelled and deveined
½ pound mushrooms, sliced ¼-inch thick
1 teaspoon Oriental sesame oil

1. Bring a large pot of water to a boil and add the snow peas; cook for exactly 20 seconds; scoop them out with a slotted spoon. Add the celery and remove after 30 seconds. Add the broccoli and remove after 1 minute. Drain well.
2. In a small bowl, combine the chicken stock and cornstarch, stirring until smooth. Stir in the sherry, soy sauce and sugar.
3. Place a large heavy wok or Dutch oven over high heat for 2 minutes. Add the vegetable oil and swirl it to coat the pan. Add the ginger and chile pepper and stir-fry for 10 seconds. Add the garlic and stir-fry for 5 seconds. Add the shrimp and stir-fry for 2 minutes. Add the mushrooms and stir-fry for a few seconds. Dump in the blanched vegetables. Stir the sauce and add it to the wok. Bring to a boil, stirring, until the sauce thickens, 1 to 2 minutes. Remove from the heat and stir in the sesame oil. Serve immediately.

Calories 279 *Protein* 34 gm *Fat* 8 gm *Carbohydrate* 19 gm *Sodium* 966 mg *Cholesterol* 211 mg

Broiled Marinated Chicken with Vegetables (page 145)

Red and Green Roasted Pepper Lasagne (page 71)

Cheese Enchiladas (page 88)

Zesty Lemon Cake Roll (page 183)

COQUILLES ST. JACQUES

This favorite French scallop gratin is prepared here without all the usual butter and cream. It is best served in real scallop shells, but small gratin dishes will work as well. The scallops are particularly good with the Three-Grain Pilaf with Mushrooms or Wild Rice and Pecan Pilaf (pages 118 and 122), although you should eliminate the mushrooms from either recipe, since this dish calls for mushrooms, too. Sliced tomatoes are good alongside.

MAKES 8 SERVINGS

1 tablespoon butter
¼ cup minced white and light green part of scallions, or shallots
1 cup dry white wine
½ bay leaf
¼ teaspoon dried basil, crumbled
1½ pounds small whole bay scallops or quartered sea scallops
½ pound mushrooms, thinly sliced
1 large egg yolk
¼ cup heavy cream
3 tablespoons all-purpose flour
¼ cup grated Swiss or Parmesan cheese (1 ounce)
Lemon wedges and parsley sprigs, for garnish

1. Preheat the broiler. Melt the butter in a large heavy saucepan over moderate heat. Add the scallions and sauté to soften, 1 to 2 minutes. Add the white wine, ½ cup water, the bay leaf and basil and bring to a boil. Add the scallops and mushrooms and return to a boil; scoop out with a slotted spoon (or drain and reserve the cooking liquid). You will have about 4 cups of liquid. Return the liquid to the heat and boil over high heat until reduced to 1¼ cups, 5 to 8 minutes. Discard the bay leaf.

2. In a medium bowl, whisk together the egg yolk, heavy cream and flour. Gradually whisk in the reduced cooking stock and turn into a small heavy saucepan. Bring to a boil, stirring or whisking constantly, over moderate heat. Reduce the heat and simmer for 1 or 2 minutes.

3. Spoon about ½ cup of the scallops and mushrooms into each of 8 individual scallop shells or gratin dishes. Spoon about 3 tablespoons of the sauce over each and top with the cheese, dividing it equally among them. Working in batches, broil until bubbly and browned, 2 to 3 minutes. Serve hot with lemon wedges and parsley sprigs.

Calories 154 *Protein* 17 gm *Fat* 7 gm *Carbohydrate* 6 gm *Sodium* 168 mg *Cholesterol* 80 mg

---

ITALIAN STUFFED SQUID *Fresh squid is one of the tastiest treats* and *best bargains in the fish market. Take care to get squid of equal size, and make sure they are cleaned before you buy them.*

*MAKES 4 MAIN-COURSE OR 8
FIRST-COURSE SERVINGS*

*8 medium-large (5 to 6-inch) squid,
    cleaned (about 1 pound)*
1 large egg
¼ cup plain dry bread crumbs
2 tablespoons olive oil
*½ cup chopped parsley (preferably
    Italian flat-leaf)*
*¼ cup freshly grated Parmesan cheese
    (1 ounce)*
1 small garlic clove, minced (optional)
½ teaspoon dried oregano, crumbled
¼ teaspoon salt
⅛ teaspoon black pepper
¾ cup dry white wine
Parsley sprigs, for garnish

1. Rinse the squid under cool running water and pat dry with paper towels. Finely chop the tentacles with a knife or in a food processor; you should have ⅔ cup.

2. In a medium bowl, stir together the chopped squid tentacles with the egg and bread crumbs. Stir in 1 tablespoon of the olive oil along with the parsley, Parmesan, garlic, oregano, salt, pepper and 1 teaspoon of the wine.

3. Using 2 to 2½ tablespoons of stuffing for each, stuff the squid, using a small spoon or a pastry bag fitted with a plain ½-inch tip. Do not fill them completely; leave about 1 inch to allow for expansion of the stuffing. Close the top with 2 crossed toothpicks or sew up with dark colored thread. (Be sure to put the needle away immediately after using it near food.)

4. Spoon the remaining 1 tablespoon olive oil into a heavy medium skillet and place over moderately high heat. Add all of the stuffed squid and brown well on one side, 2 to 3 minutes. Turn and lightly brown on the other side. Add the remaining white wine and bring to a boil. Cover, reduce the heat and simmer until tender, 30 to 40 minutes. Remove the squid with a slotted spoon and measure the cooking liquid; there should be ¼ cup. If there is more, boil it until reduced to ¼ cup. If there is less, add water to make ¼ cup.

5. Remove the toothpicks or strings. Cut the stuffed squid crosswise into ½-inch slices and overlap them on plates. Spoon 1 tablespoon of the cooking liquid over each main-course serving, or divide it equally for first-course servings. Garnish with the parsley sprigs.

NOTE: Nutritional values given below refer to a main-course serving of 2 squid.

Calories 242 **Protein** *23 gm* **Fat** *12 gm* **Carbohydrate** *10 gm* **Sodium** *367 mg* **Cholesterol** *338 mg*

SEAFOOD SUKIYAKI *This festive Japanese one-pot dinner, calling here for seafood rather than the traditional beef, is perfect, even dramatic, for special occasions. The several ingredients not generally found in the supermarket can be obtained from any source that sells Japanese ingredients. You may wish to substitute extra seafood or fish for the live lobster; the results will be just as spectacular. If you do not have a flameproof casserole and burner to cook with at the table, consider using an electric skillet or cooking the sukiyaki in the kitchen.*

MAKES 6 SERVINGS

2 quarts dashi *(light seafood stock; recipe follows)*

5 slices fresh ginger, each the size of a quarter

1/2 cup sake *(Japanese rice wine)*

1/3 cup mirin *(sweet rice wine)*

1/4 cup reduced-sodium Japanese soy sauce

1 large (2-pound) live lobster, (or an extra 1/2 pound shrimp, scallops or fish)

12 medium-size dried shiitake mushrooms (1 1/2 ounces), or 12 fresh shiitake mushrooms

12 pieces fu *(wheat gluten)*, each about 1 inch *(optional)*

3 ounces soba *(whole wheat-buckwheat noodles)*

1/2 pound fresh white mushrooms, sliced

1/2 pound Napa cabbage, shredded (3 cups)

1/2 pound fresh spinach, cut into 1-inch-wide ribbons

1/2 pound fresh bean sprouts

12 medium scallions, trimmed, cut on severe angle into 2-inch lengths

1 cake (6-ounce) grilled tofu (yakidofu) or plain soft bean curd, cut into 12 cubes

18 medium shrimp (1/2 pound), shelled and deveined

1/2 pound sea scallops, quartered, or whole bay scallops

1/2 pound fresh tuna or swordfish, cut into 3/4-inch cubes

1. Pour the *dashi* into a large nonreactive saucepan. Add the ginger, *sake, mirin* and soy sauce. Reserve.

2. Kill the lobster by piercing it lengthwise at the center of the cross-shaped mark behind its head with a large heavy knife. Split the entire lobster lengthwise after it has stopped kicking. Scoop out the tail meat. Spoon out and reserve the liver (tomally) which is dark green and the roe (if present) which is grey-green. Crack the claws with a nutcracker or mallet and scoop out the flesh. Cut all of the lobster meat into 3/4-inch pieces and reserve. Rinse the shells and add to the *dashi* (if not using lobster, add shrimp shells). Place over moderate heat and bring to a boil. Reduce the heat and simmer for 10 minutes. Drain, discarding the solids; strain.

3. Pour 2 cups hot water over the shiitake in a medium bowl and let soak for

about 1 hour to soften. Drain. Cut out and discard the tough stems. If using fresh shiitake, simply slice off the stems; do not soak. If desired, cut out decorative Xs in the top center of each cap, using a paring knife to make each groove. Strain the soaking liquid into the *dashi*.

4. Place the *fu* in a small bowl and add 1 cup of cold water. Let soak for 5 minutes to soften. Drain and gently squeeze out excess water.

5. Pour about 2 quarts of water into a large saucepan and bring to a boil over high heat. Drop in the *soba* and bring to a boil, stirring constantly. Pour in ½ cup cold water to stop the boil. Return to a boil. Again, pour in ½ cup cold water to stop the boil. Return to a boil and cook, stirring frequently, until firm but tender. Drain; rinse under cold water and drain again.

6. On 1 or 2 large platters or trays, ar-range the lobster, shiitake, *fu, soba*, sliced fresh mushrooms, Napa cabbage, spinach, bean sprouts, scallions, tofu, shrimp, scallops and tuna or swordfish. (This can also be done on individual plates if you prefer.)

7. Pour half the flavored *dashi* into a large sukiyaki pot, flameproof shallow casserole or electric skillet and bring to a boil on a burner at the table. Guests use chopsticks to dip the ingredients into simmering stock to cook and then transfer them to a small plate to eat. To cook the tomally and roe, lower it in with a large spoon or ladle for a minute. Serve small soup bowls alongside for the tasty broth. Ingredients take only 1 to 2 minutes to cook. When the broth gets low, pour in the rest and bring to a boil. Continue dipping and eating in this manner.

NOTE: Nutritional values given below are inclusive of ingredients for *dashi* (recipe on following page).

Calories 349	*Protein* 40 gm	*Fat* 5 gm	*Carbohydrate* 34 gm	*Sodium* 858 mg	*Cholesterol* 103 mg

DASHI (LIGHT SEAFOOD STOCK) *When ordering the Japanese ingredients for the Seafood Sukiyaki be sure to order the shaved* bonito *and* konbu *(kelp) for making this important stock. To save time and effort, you may wish to use one of the instant* dashi *mixes in place of the following recipe.*

MAKES 2 QUARTS

2 lengths (20 inches each) dashi konbu
   (dried sea kelp)
3 cups (2 ounces) loosely packed shaved
   bonito (katsuo bushi)

1. Combine 2½ quarts of cold water and *konbu* in a large heavy soup pot, stockpot or saucepan and place over moderate heat. Bring to a boil that takes about 10 minutes to reach (do not speed up). Pierce a piece of *konbu* with a finger nail; it should pierce easily when sufficient flavor has been released into the broth. Do not boil. Remove and discard the *konbu* and then bring the liquid to a full boil. Add ½ cup cold water to lower the temperature.

2. Dump in all of the shaved *bonito*. Do not stir. Bring first to a full boil. Remove from the heat *immediately*. Allow to settle for about 1 minute. Line a colander with several layers of damp cheesecloth and place over a large bowl. Strain the *dashi*. Discard the solids (but do not squeeze). The *dashi* is ready to use. It can be cooled to room temperature and then chilled for 1 day.

NOTE: Nutritional values given below are per cup serving.

Calories 13   **Protein** *1 gm*   *Fat* *0 gm*   **Carbohydrate** *2 gm*   **Sodium** *125 mg*   **Cholesterol** *4 mg*

OYSTERS AU GRATIN *These oysters on the half shell are lightly coated with a creamy sauce and sprinkled with Parmesan cheese before broiling. They are perfect when served with the Cornbread- and Tasso-Stuffed Artichokes on page 107, and also make great hors d'oeuvres.*

MAKES 4 SERVINGS

32 oysters—shucked, 32 shell halves scrubbed and dried and ½ cup oyster liquor reserved
1 cup milk
1 garlic clove, minced
¼ teaspoon freshly grated nutmeg
¼ cup all-purpose flour
½ teaspoon Tabasco or hot pepper sauce
2 tablespoons freshly grated Parmesan cheese
4 small limes, cut into wedges, for garnish

1. In a large heavy skillet, bring ¼-inch of water to a simmer over moderate heat. Add the oysters in 2 or 3 batches and poach until the edges just begin to curl, about 1 minute. Remove with a skimmer or a slotted spoon; drain on paper towels.

2. Preheat the broiler. In a medium saucepan, combine the milk, ½ cup reserved oyster liquor, garlic and nutmeg. Hold a sieve over the pan and add the flour to the sieve. Gently tap the sieve once and gradually whisk the flour into the liquid. Repeat until all of the flour is whisked in and smooth. Set over moderate heat and bring to a boil, whisking constantly. Boil, whisking, for 3 minutes. Remove from the heat and stir in the Tabasco.

3. Return the oysters to their half-shells and place on 2 baking sheets that will fit under the broiler (or do in 2 batches). Coat each oyster with about 2 teaspoons of the sauce and a generous pinch of the Parmesan cheese. Broil the oysters about 4 inches from the heat until the sauce is bubbly and speckled brown, 2 to 3 minutes. Serve hot, with lime wedges on the side.

Calories *160*   **Protein** *12 gm*   **Fat** *6 gm*   **Carbohydrate** *14 gm*   **Sodium** *218 mg*   **Cholesterol** *73 mg*

MUSTARD CHICKEN *The pungent fragrance of this mustard-coated chicken will draw everyone to the kitchen as it cooks. This is a good choice for a make-ahead dinner or picnic.*

MAKES 6 SERVINGS

12 medium-size skinless chicken thighs
(2 to 2¼ pounds total weight)
½ cup low-sodium mustard (recipe
follows) or Dijon mustard
2 English muffins (2 ounces each)
2 teaspoons paprika
½ teaspoon dried tarragon, crumbled
½ teaspoon black pepper
1 large whole egg
1 egg white
1½ tablespoons melted butter
3 tablespoons fresh lemon juice

1. In a large bowl, combine the mustard with the chicken and toss to coat. Let marinate at room temperature for 30 minutes.

2. Preheat the oven to 375°. Tear up the English muffins and grind them into fresh bread crumbs in a food processor or by hand. Toss them in a medium bowl with the paprika, tarragon and pepper.

3. In a shallow dish or pie plate, whisk together the egg, egg white and 1 teaspoon water.

4. Lightly oil a 13-by-9-inch baking pan or shallow casserole (or lightly spray with nonstick vegetable spray). One at a time, dip the pieces of mustard-coated chicken in the egg mixture, then roll in the seasoned crumbs. Use fewer crumbs on the underside since chicken pieces will not be turned during cooking (it's best to make the tops look nicest). Place close together in a single layer in the baking dish.

5. Stir together the melted butter and lemon juice in a cup. Spoon over the chicken. Bake, uncovered, in the center of the oven for 50 to 60 minutes, until deep golden brown and crispy on top and cooked through. When done, the juices will run clear when the chicken is pierced with a fork. Let stand for 10 to 15 minutes. Serve hot or at room temperature.

NOTE: Nutritional values given below are inclusive of all ingredients in Low-Sodium Mustard (recipe on following page).

Calories *289*   **Protein** *25 gm*   **Fat** *13 gm*   **Carbohydrate** *18 gm*   **Sodium** *238 mg*   **Cholesterol** *140 mg*

LOW-SODIUM MUSTARD

MAKES ABOUT ½ CUP

3 tablespoons yellow mustard seeds
2 tablespoons powdered mustard
1 teaspoon turmeric
1 teaspoon dried tarragon, crumbled
¼ teaspoon ground cinnamon
¼ cup cider vinegar
¼ cup dry white wine
2 tablespoons sugar
1 tablespoon olive oil
1 garlic clove, minced or crushed
  through a press

1. In a small nonreactive saucepan, combine the mustard seeds, powdered mustard, turmeric, tarragon and cinnamon. Stir in ⅔ cup warm water. Stirring constantly, bring to a boil over moderate heat. Remove from the heat, cover and let stand at room temperature for 8 hours or overnight.

2. Uncover the pan and stir in the vinegar, wine, sugar, olive oil and garlic. Bring to a boil, stirring, over moderate heat. Reduce the heat to low and simmer, stirring frequently, for 5 minutes. Let cool slightly. Purée the mixture in a food processor or blender. Let cool to room temperature and use, or cover and chill for as long as 2 weeks.

NOTE: Nutritional values given below are per teaspoon serving.

Calories 19   **Protein** *1 gm*   **Fat** *1 gm*   **Carbohydrate** *2 gm*   **Sodium** *0 mg*   **Cholesterol** *0 mg*

BROILED MARINATED CHICKEN WITH VEGE-TABLES *The marinade paste used to season the chicken here is a* Mexican recado: *The chicken should marinate for at least 12 hours. The wonderful, slightly charred flavor of grilled vegetables is achieved under the broiler with little fuss or mess. The flavors improve if the vegetables are cooked several hours ahead, leaving just the marinated chicken to be broiled at dinnertime.*

MAKES 4 SERVINGS

5 large unpeeled garlic cloves
½ teaspoon salt
1 teaspoon black pepper
½ teaspoon dried oregano, crumbled
½ teaspoon ground cumin
⅛ teaspoon ground cloves
2 tablespoons fresh lime juice
4 small (4-ounce) skinless boned chicken breast halves
2 medium (6-ounce) green bell peppers
4 medium (6-ounce) zucchini, trimmed and halved lengthwise
4 very small (4-ounce) eggplants, trimmed and halved lengthwise
4 small (2-ounce) onions, peeled and halved crosswise, plus ½ cup finely chopped onion
4 small (3-ounce) plum tomatoes, halved lengthwise
1 tablespoon vegetable oil
2 teaspoons all-purpose flour
1 cup canned chicken broth or stock
¼ cup dry white wine
¼ cup chopped fresh parsley
Salt

1. Place the unpeeled garlic cloves on a heavy griddle or in a cast-iron skillet over moderate heat and toast, turning frequently, until spotted dark brown on the outside and soft inside, 15 to 20 minutes. Let cool slightly. Peel and chop on a cutting board. Add the salt and, using the side of a knife blade, work into a paste.
2. Scrape the garlic paste into a small bowl and stir in the black pepper, oregano, cumin and ground cloves. Gradually stir in the lime juice. Spread this seasoning paste all over the chicken breast halves; wrap tightly and refrigerate for 12 to 24 hours.
3. Roast the green peppers directly over a gas flame or under the broiler as close to the heat as possible, turning until charred all over. Place in a plastic bag and let steam for 5 minutes in the refrigerator. Working over a colander, peel the peppers under gently running warm water. Remove the cores and seeds; cut the pepper into ½-inch strips.
4. Preheat the broiler. Deeply score the cut sides of the zucchini and the eggplants in diagonal lines about ½-inch apart. Working in 2 batches, if necessary, arrange the zucchini, eggplants, halved onions and tomatoes in a single layer on a foil-lined broiler pan. Brush the zuc-

chini, eggplants, onions and tomatoes with 2 teaspoons of the vegetable oil. Broil about 4 inches from the heat until the vegetables are slightly blackened on top and soft and tender inside, 5 to 15 minutes. Remove, cover with aluminum foil and set aside.

5. Let the chicken return to room temperature before broiling. Remove the chicken from the marinade; reserve the marinade for the sauce. Broil the chicken on a foil-lined broiler pan until speckled dark brown on top, 3 to 5 minutes. Turn and broil until just cooked through, 1 to 3 minutes longer. Wrap in aluminum foil to keep warm and pour any drippings into the reserved marinade.

6. Put the remaining 1 teaspoon vege-

table oil in a small heavy skillet, preferably nonstick. Add the ½ cup chopped onion and sauté over moderate heat until lightly colored, 3 to 5 minutes. Add the flour and cook, stirring, for 1 minute. Whisk in the reserved marinade, the chicken broth and the wine. Bring to a boil, whisking, until thickened slightly. Simmer, stirring frequently, until reduced to 1 cup, about 5 minutes. Remove from the heat and stir in the parsley. Season with salt to taste.

7. To serve, thinly slice the chicken breasts across the grain and fan out (overlap) in the center of each dinner plate. Divide the vegetables among the plates; drizzle the sauce over the chicken and vegetables. Serve warm or at room temperature.

Calories 286 **Protein** 33 gm **Fat** 6 gm **Carbohydrate** 28 gm **Sodium** 621 mg **Cholesterol** 66 mg

CHICKEN JAMBALAYA WITH RAINBOW CREOLE SAUCE

Just one-half pound of chicken is enough for six generous servings when teamed with plenty of fresh vegetables and rice. The cooking technique has been simplified and this dish is a cinch to put together. Be sure to have all of the ingredients ready before you start to cook. This is also delicious without the Creole sauce (which contributes 44 of the 316 calories in this dish).

MAKES 6 SERVINGS

JAMBALAYA:

- 1 tablespoon vegetable oil
- 1¼ cups long-grain white rice
- 2 cups chopped onion
- 1½ cups finely diced celery
- 1 cup finely diced green bell pepper
- 1 large garlic clove, minced
- 3 ounces Canadian bacon, cut into ¼-inch-wide strips
- ½ teaspoon cayenne pepper
- ½ teaspoon ground cumin
- ½ teaspoon dried basil, crumbled
- ½ teaspoon dried thyme, crumbled
- ½ teaspoon paprika
- ½ teaspoon black pepper
- 1 bay leaf, or ½ California bay laurel leaf
- 1 cup canned tomatoes, seeded, drained and coarsely chopped
- ½ cup tomato juice (drained from above)
- 1 cup canned chicken broth or stock
- ½ pound skinless boned chicken breast, thinly sliced across the grain

RAINBOW CREOLE SAUCE:

- 1 tablespoon butter
- ½ cup chopped onion
- ½ cup finely diced red bell pepper
- ½ cup finely diced yellow bell pepper
- ½ cup finely diced green bell pepper
- 1 large garlic clove, minced or crushed through a press
- 1 cup canned tomatoes, seeded, drained and coarsely chopped
- ½ cup tomato juice (drained from above)
- ½ teaspoon dried basil, crumbled
- ⅛ teaspoon dried oregano, crumbled
- ⅛ teaspoon ground cumin
- ⅛ teaspoon cayenne pepper
- 1 bay leaf, or ½ California bay laurel leaf
- ½ teaspoon sugar
- 2 teaspoons fresh lemon juice
- Salt and pepper

1. PREPARE THE JAMBALAYA: In a heavy medium saucepan combine the vegetable oil and rice. Stir over moderate heat until the grains are opaque and golden brown, 3 to 4 minutes.

2. Add the onion, celery, green bell pepper and garlic and cook, stirring, for

147

about 3 minutes to soften the vegetables slightly. Add the Canadian bacon and cook for 1 minute longer. Stir in the cayenne, cumin, basil, thyme, paprika, black pepper and bay leaf. Cook for about 30 seconds and stir in the tomatoes, tomato juice and chicken stock. Bring to a simmer and stir in the chicken. Bring to a boil, stirring once or twice. Cover, reduce the heat to low and simmer, stirring gently once or twice, until the rice is tender and the liquid absorbed, 15 to 18 minutes. Uncover and cook for 1 minute longer. Let stand for 10 to 15 minutes before serving.

3. PREPARE THE RAINBOW CREOLE SAUCE: Melt the butter in a small nonreactive saucepan over moderate heat. Add the onion and the red, yellow and green peppers and sauté to soften, 3 to 5 minutes. Add the garlic and cook for 30 seconds longer. Stir in the tomatoes, tomato juice, basil, oregano, cumin, cayenne, bay leaf, sugar and lemon juice. Bring to a boil. Reduce the heat and simmer for 3 to 5 minutes to blend the flavors. Add a pinch each of salt and pepper to taste. Serve hot, about ⅓ cup per serving, spooning it over or alongside the jambalaya.

Calories 316   *Protein* 17 gm   *Fat* 7 gm   *Carbohydrate* 47 gm   *Sodium* 639 mg   *Cholesterol* 34 mg

---

CHICKEN SOONG

This is a dish of finely diced stir-fried ingredients that are wrapped into little parcels of romaine lettuce and eaten with one's fingers. They can be assembled at the table by guests or you can make them ahead. They are good cold, and carry nicely to picnics. Chicken Soong also makes a good hors d'oeuvre.

MAKES 6 SERVINGS

1 pound skinless boned chicken breasts, cut in ½-inch cubes
2 tablespoons reduced-sodium soy sauce
1 tablespoon rice wine or dry sherry
1 tablespoon rice vinegar
1 tablespoon cornstarch
1 teaspoon sugar
24 large romaine lettuce leaves (start with 2 heads)
¼ cup finely chopped walnuts (1 ounce)
1 tablespoon peanut oil or vegetable oil
1 tablespoon minced fresh ginger
1 medium garlic clove, minced or crushed through a press
1 medium-large (6-ounce) red bell pepper, finely diced
½ pound fresh mushrooms, cut in ¼-inch dice
1 cup finely diced water chestnuts (see NOTE)
1 can (8-ounce) sliced bamboo shoots, finely diced
⅓ cup canned chicken broth or stock
½ cup sliced scallions
3 tablespoons chopped cilantro (fresh coriander)

NOTE: It is best to use fresh water chestnuts (see instructions following this recipe). If not available, use one 8-ounce can, drained.

1. In a medium glass bowl, combine the chicken, soy sauce, rice wine, rice vinegar, cornstarch and sugar. Stir together and let marinate at room temperature for 30 minutes.

2. Bring a large pot of water to a boil. One at a time, dip the romaine lettuce leaves into the water for 3 to 5 seconds to soften. Drain in a colander. With a paring knife, slice off the raised portion of the thick vein at the base of each leaf. Stack the leaves until needed.

3. Heat a large heavy wok over moderately high heat. Add the walnuts and toast for 1 to 2 minutes. Remove and reserve.

4. Heat the wok over high heat and add the peanut oil. It may be necessary to regulate the heat from moderate to high as you work (if it smokes, lower the heat a little but cook over the highest heat possible). Add the ginger and garlic and cook for 10 seconds. Add the red bell pepper and stir-fry for 30 seconds. Add the mushrooms and stir-fry for 30 seconds longer. Add the water chestnuts and bamboo shoots and stir-fry for 30 seconds longer. Add the chicken and the chicken broth; cook for about 2 minutes,

just until the chicken is cooked through and the sauce is thickened. Stir in the scallions and the reserved walnuts and cook for 10 seconds. Remove from the heat and stir in the cilantro.

5. To assemble, spoon about ¼ cup of the filling onto the lower third of each lettuce leaf. Fold the stem end up over the filling; fold the sides in over the filling and roll up. If assembling ahead, place seam-side down on the dishes or platter.

FRESH WATER CHESTNUTS
Fresh water chestnuts are light years ahead of canned ones in terms of freshness and flavor. They are not always available, but check in any local Oriental market: They look somewhat like squat gladiola bulbs. One pound will yield only 8 to 10 ounces after peeling. One cup, sliced, will weigh about 5 ounces after cooking and draining.

Choose firm water chestnuts without soft spots. They are imported from China, so some are bound to be spoiled. Slice off the top and bottom and peel with a paring knife, dropping them into a saucepan filled with cold, lightly acidulated water (1 tablespoon vinegar to 1 quart of water). Set the pan over moderate heat and bring to a boil. Cook for 5 minutes. Drop the water chestnuts into cold water and let cool. Slice when cool.

NOTE: If the Mexican tuber known as jicama is available, it makes a good substitute for fresh water chestnuts (use it raw, as is; do not cook).

Calories 199   *Protein* 21 gm   *Fat* 7 gm   *Carbohydrate* 14 gm   *Sodium* 262 mg   *Cholesterol* 44 mg

AROMATIC CHICKEN CURRY WITH TWO FRESH CHUTNEYS

Deep spicy flavors in the chicken's rich and plentiful curry sauce are complemented by the Fragrant Basmati Rice Timbales on page 119. Serve cubes of fresh mango (1/4 cup has 27 calories) or the Fresh Mango Chutney (page 152) or Peach Chutney with Pecans (page 153) on the plate alongside the curry and timbale.

MAKES 4 SERVINGS

1 tablespoon vegetable oil
1 medium (4-ounce) onion, finely chopped
1 tablespoon minced fresh ginger
1 large garlic clove, minced or crushed
   through a press
2 teaspoons garam masala (see NOTE),
   or 1 teaspoon curry powder mixed with
   $\frac{1}{2}$ teaspoon ground coriander,
   $\frac{1}{2}$ teaspoon ground cumin and a dash
   of cayenne pepper
1 teaspoon curry powder
8 whole cardamom pods
8 whole cloves
2 tablespoons all-purpose flour
2 cups canned chicken broth or stock
$\frac{3}{4}$ pound skinless boned chicken
   breasts, cut crosswise on the diagonal
   into $\frac{1}{8}$- to $\frac{1}{4}$-inch-thick slices
$\frac{1}{2}$ cup plain lowfat yogurt
2 tablespoons chopped cilantro (fresh
   coriander)
Pinch of cayenne pepper
$\frac{1}{4}$ teaspoon salt
1 large mango or 1 small papaya, cut
   into $\frac{1}{2}$-inch dice, or Fresh Mango
   Chutney (page 152) or Peach Chutney
   with Pecans (page 153) for garnish

NOTE: Available at Indian groceries and specialty food shops.

1. In a heavy medium saucepan, warm the oil over moderate heat. Add the onion, ginger and garlic. Cook until the onion is soft and lightly colored, about 5 minutes. Add the garam masala, curry powder, cardamon pods and whole cloves. Cook, stirring, for 1 minute. Add the flour and stir to moisten with the oil; the mixture will be dry. Cook, stirring, for 1 minute. Gradually whisk in the chicken broth and bring to a boil, stirring constantly. Simmer for 15 minutes. If desired, remove the cardamom pods and cloves with a skimmer.

2. Add the chicken slices and yogurt and cook until the chicken is just cooked through, 3 to 5 minutes. Remove from the heat and stir in the cilantro, cayenne and salt. Spoon one-fourth of the curry onto each dinner plate. Garnish with the mango or peach chutney. Serve with Fragrant Basmati Rice Timbales.

Calories 189   *Protein* 23 gm   *Fat* 6 gm   *Carbohydrate* 9 gm   *Sodium* 715 mg   *Cholesterol* 51 mg

FRESH MANGO CHUTNEY *This cool, refreshing chutney is far better than any of the bottled varieties. It is excellent served with the Aromatic Chicken Curry or with the Beef with Spicy Spinach Sauce on page 164.*

MAKES ABOUT 2 CUPS (32 SERVINGS OF 1 TABLESPOON EACH)

1/4 cup packed light brown sugar
1/4 cup distilled white vinegar
1/4 cup raisins
5 whole cloves
1/2 teaspoon freshly grated nutmeg
1/4 teaspoon ground cinnamon
1/4 teaspoon salt
1 small (2-ounce) onion, finely chopped
2 cups coarsely chopped firm ripe mango
2 tablespoons fresh lemon juice

1. In a medium nonreactive saucepan, combine the brown sugar, vinegar, raisins, cloves, nutmeg, cinnamon, salt and onion. Bring to a boil, stirring, over moderate heat. Reduce the heat and simmer, stirring frequently, for 5 minutes.

2. Add the mango and 2 tablespoons water. Simmer, stirring frequently, until thickened, about 5 minutes. Remove from the heat and stir in the lemon juice. Let cool to room temperature. Cover and refrigerate for at least 2 hours or up to 1 week. Serve chilled or at room temperature.

Calories *18*   **Protein** *0 gm*   **Fat** *0 gm*   **Carbohydrate** *5 gm*   **Sodium** *18 mg*   **Cholesterol** *0 mg*

Peach Chutney with Pecans *Use fresh ripe peaches to make this simple, intense chutney. It is a perfect complement to the Aromatic Chicken Curry (page 151) or the Beef with Spicy Spinach Sauce on page 164.*

MAKES ABOUT 1 CUP (16 SERVINGS OF 1 TABLESPOON EACH)

2 cups coarsely chopped peeled ripe peaches
¼ cup honey
2 tablespoons plus 1 teaspoon minced fresh ginger
1 cinnamon stick (3-inch)
2 tablespoons fresh lemon juice
3 tablespoons finely chopped pecans
⅛ teaspoon almond extract

1. In a medium nonreactive saucepan, combine the peaches, honey, 2 tablespoons of the ginger, the cinnamon stick and lemon juice. Bring to a boil over moderate heat, stirring once in a while. Reduce the heat and simmer, stirring frequently, until the syrup is reduced and slightly thickened, about 10 minutes.

2. Remove from the heat and stir in the pecans, almond extract and the remaining 1 teaspoon ginger. Let cool to room temperature. Cover and refrigerate for at least 2 hours or up to 3 or 4 days. Serve chilled or at room temperature.

Calories *35* **Protein** *.3 gm* **Fat** *1 gm* **Carbohydrate** *7 gm* **Sodium** *.4 mg* **Cholesterol** *0 mg*

CHICKEN TACOS

These are tacos suaves, *soft tacos, with soft steamed corn tortillas rather than crisp calorie-laden fried ones. In Mexico tacos are street food, to be eaten immediately after assembling them. To enjoy them at their best, it is a good idea to heat, assemble and eat them as you go.*

MAKES 4 SERVINGS OF
2 TACOS EACH

CHICKEN FILLING:
  1 large (1½-pound) whole chicken
    breast, halved
  1 large garlic clove, minced or crushed
    through a press

TACOS:
  8 fresh corn tortillas (6-inch diameter)
  1 cup diced tomato
  1 cup shredded romaine lettuce
  4 tablespoons chopped cilantro (fresh
    coriander) (optional)
  ½ cup mild taco sauce
  ½ cup shredded mild Cheddar cheese
    (2 ounces)
  Hot pepper sauce, such as Chipotle, to
    taste (optional)
  Salt

1. MAKE THE CHICKEN FILLING: Pull the skin off the chicken and discard it. Put the chicken in a heavy medium saucepan along with the garlic and 1 cup of cold water. Partially cover and bring to a boil over moderate heat. Reduce the heat and simmer until almost cooked through, about 15 minutes. Remove the chicken to a plate until cool enough to handle. Meanwhile, boil the broth from the chicken over moderate heat until reduced to ½ cup, 5 to 7 minutes.

2. Tear the chicken meat from the bones (it's okay if it's slightly pink because it will finish cooking in the broth) and tear it into shreds, pulling in the direction of the grain. Put the shreds into the reduced broth. Bring to a boil and simmer for 1 to 2 minutes to blend the flavors and complete the cooking.

3. MAKE THE TACOS: Place a heavy skillet or griddle over moderate heat. When hot, heat the tortillas 1 or 2 at a time. Put 1 tortilla in the skillet; dip your fingers in water and flick the water drops onto the tortilla; turn and repeat. (If they are very fresh and pliable they will not need water; most will be somewhat stiff and require a few splashes of water to make them soft and fresh again.) Do not heat too much or they may dry out. With experience you can do this right on an open gas flame as I do, and skip the skillet. The idea is to reconstitute them so they are as soft and supple as when freshly made.

4. Place 1 hot corn tortilla on a plate. Spoon 3 tablespoons of the chicken filling across the center. Top with 2 tablespoons of tomato, 2 tablespoons shredded lettuce, ½ tablespoon of chopped cilantro, 1 tablespoon taco sauce, 1 tablespoon Cheddar, a splash of hot pepper sauce and a pinch of salt. Repeat to make 8 tacos, 2 per serving. Serve hot. To eat, fold the tortilla over the filling and eat with your fingers.

Calories *338*   **Protein** *34 gm*   **Fat** *8 gm*   **Carbohydrate** *31 gm*   **Sodium** *491 mg*   **Cholesterol** *79 mg*

CHICKEN AND VEGETABLE YAKITORI *Four ounces of chicken breast is enough to make two skewers per serving when teamed with vegetables. You can broil these in the oven, but I urge you to charcoal broil them on a grill. Any pilaf or rice dish would make a good accompaniment with sliced tomatoes or cherry tomatoes alongside.*

MAKES 4 SERVINGS

1 cup sake *(Japanese rice wine)*
2 tablespoons reduced-sodium soy sauce
2 tablespoons sugar
5 slices of fresh ginger, each the size of a quarter
1 large garlic clove, sliced
1 pound skinless boned chicken breasts, cut lengthwise into 24 ½-inch-wide strips
8 small white onions (½ pound)
1 large (8-ounce) green bell pepper, quartered, seeds and ribs removed
8 large mushrooms (about ½ pound)

1. In a nonreactive small saucepan, combine the *sake,* soy sauce, sugar, ginger and garlic. Bring to a boil over moderate heat. Reduce the heat and simmer until reduced to ⅔ cup, about 10 minutes. Pour into a medium bowl and let cool to room temperature. Remove and discard the ginger and garlic. The yield will now be ½ cup. Add the chicken strips and let marinate while you start a charcoal fire or preheat the broiler.

2. Meanwhile, bring a medium-large pot of water to a boil over high heat. Drop in the unpeeled onions and when the water returns to a boil, boil for 5 minutes. Cut each pepper quarter into 4 pieces. Drop them in with the onions and boil for 2 minutes after the boil returns.

Drain and set aside until cool enough to handle. When cool, trim the ends of the onions and peel them.

3. When the coals are hot and covered in gray ash, heat the grill itself. The broiler, if using, should preheat for 10 to 15 minutes.

4. You will need eight 12-inch metal or bamboo skewers. Thread the ingredients onto them in the following order: Push the point through the rounded center of a mushroom cap and pull it to within 1 inch of the blunt end of the skewer (work assembly-line fashion, i.e. put each of the 8 mushrooms on its skewer (first). Weave or thread 1 strip of chicken on each skewer, making an s-shape (so the meat is pierced 3 times before sliding up next to the mushroom). Next, add a piece of bell pepper, then a strip of chicken, then a whole onion, jabbed sideways, followed by another strip of chicken and finally, a piece of bell pepper.

5. Place the skewers on the hot grill and brush with the marinade left in the bowl. Cook, turning and brushing 4 to 6 times, until browned and cooked through, about 15 minutes. Or cook under the broiler for 10 to 15 minutes, until cooked through. Serve hot or at room temperature.

Calories *206*   **Protein** *29 gm*   **Fat** *2 gm*   **Carbohydrate** *18 gm*   **Sodium** *387 mg*   **Cholesterol** *66 mg*

BROILED FETA CHICKEN *Minestrone (page 32) or Fresh Tomato-Cilantro Soup (page 26) make good beginnings to this zesty entrée. This dish is also good cold or at room temperature, so leftovers won't go to waste.*

MAKES 4 SERVINGS

1 cup plain lowfat yogurt
1 medium garlic clove, minced or
crushed through a press
½ teaspoon dried rosemary, crumbled
¼ teaspoon black pepper
4 skinless boned chicken breast halves
(5 ounces each)
½ cup crumbled feta cheese (2 ounces)

1. In a shallow dish or glass pie pan, stir together the yogurt, garlic, rosemary and pepper. Add the chicken breasts, turn to coat, and marinate in the refrigerator for 1 to 3 hours. Let come to room temperature for 30 minutes before cooking. Remove the chicken from the marinade; reserve any marinade in the dish.

2. Preheat the broiler. Line a broiler pan with aluminum foil and arrange the breasts on it, smooth side down. Broil for 4 to 7 minutes. Turn, spoon any remaining marinade over the breasts and crumble the feta over the top. Broil until just cooked through (the juices will run clear when pierced) and lightly browned, 4 to 7 minutes longer. Serve hot.

Calories *231*   **Protein** *38 gm*   **Fat** *6 gm*   **Carbohydrate** *5 gm*   **Sodium** *290 mg*   **Cholesterol** *98 mg*

PASTEL DE POLLO *Here is a tasty Mexican-style cold chicken loaf layered with colorful red and green bell peppers. It makes a great hot weather luncheon or dinner and is especially good with the optional Tomato Yogurt in the accompanying recipe.*

MAKES 12 SERVINGS

2 large (8-ounce) red bell peppers
2 large (8-ounce) green bell peppers
¾ pound skinless boned chicken breasts
¾ pound skinless boned chicken thighs
2 large whole eggs
2 egg yolks
2 tablespoons all-purpose flour
½ cup heavy cream
½ teaspoon ground cumin
¼ teaspoon freshly grated nutmeg
¼ teaspoon black pepper
1 teaspoon Tabasco or hot pepper sauce
1 medium garlic clove, minced or
   crushed through a press
½ cup thinly sliced scallions
18 whole medium-size pitted ripe black
   olives (2 ounces)
Salt
Tomato Yogurt (optional
   accompaniment, recipe follows)
Lemon wedges, for garnish (optional)

1. Roast the peppers directly over a gas flame or under the broiler as close to the heat as possible, turning with tongs until charred all over. Place in a plastic bag, twisting the top to enclose them and put in the refrigerator for 5 to 10 minutes. Working over a colander, peel the peppers by rubbing the skins away under gently running water. Cut the peppers in half lengthwise; remove and discard the seeds, ribs and stems. Keeping the red and green peppers separate, cut lengthwise into ½-inch strips.
2. Preheat the oven to 350°. Lightly coat a 9-by-5-by-3 inch loaf pan with nonstick vegetable spray, or lightly oil. Line the pan with aluminum foil so the edges overhang the long sides by 1 inch. Spray or oil the foil. Choose a shallow roasting pan slightly larger than the loaf pan to act as a water bath.
3. Cut the chicken breasts and thighs into ¾-inch cubes. Reserve ½ cup of each. Finely grind the remaining chicken in a food processor or meat grinder.
4. In a large bowl, whisk the whole eggs with the egg yolks. Whisk in the flour, cream, cumin, nutmeg, pepper, Tabasco and garlic. Stir in the ground chicken, reserved cubed chicken, the scallions and black olives. Season with salt to taste.
5. Spoon 1 cup of the chicken mixture into the prepared loaf pan. Arrange ¼

of the pepper strips lengthwise over the chicken, making 5 rows and alternating red and green (for the remaining layers, alternate the pattern). Repeat, making 5 layers of chicken sandwiched with 4 layers of peppers. Set the loaf pan in the larger pan and add hot water to reach up the sides of the loaf pan by 1 or 2 inches. Bake for about 1 hour, or until golden brown on top and set. Let cool to room temperature on a rack. Chill for several hours or overnight. Invert the loaf onto a rectangular serving platter and peel off the aluminum foil. If desired, decorate the top with lemon slices. To serve, cut into 12 slices and spoon 2 tablespoons of the Tomato Yogurt over each.

Calories 154   *Protein* 15 gm   *Fat* 8 gm   *Carbohydrate* 5 gm   *Sodium* 100 mg   *Cholesterol* 145 mg

TOMATO YOGURT *This recipe is simplicity itself; all you do is whisk tomato paste into yogurt. The sweetness of tomato offsets the tang of the yogurt. It is also good as a dip for the Shrimp Sausages on page 19 and a dollop can be spooned into the Creamy Broccoli Soup (page 28) to dress it up.*

MAKES 1½ CUPS OR 24 SERVINGS OF 1 TABLESPOON EACH

1¼ cups plain lowfat yogurt
¼ cup tomato paste
½ teaspoon salt

1. Combine all of the ingredients in a medium bowl and whisk until evenly blended. If making ahead, cover and refrigerate.

Calories 10   *Protein* 1 gm   *Fat* 0 gm   *Carbohydrate* 1 gm   *Sodium* 75 mg   *Cholesterol* 1 mg

TURKEY SLICES WITH CREAM GRAVY *Here's a great dish for hungry dieting holiday diners without the calorie content of the whole bird. Serve with Mashed Potatoes (page 112), carrots (31 calories each), cranberry sauce (1 tablespoon has 26 calories) and a green vegetable. It is festive, colorful and comforting.*

MAKES 4 SERVINGS

1 pound skinless boned turkey breast, in one piece or thinly sliced
2 tablespoons butter
1 chicken liver (optional)
1 chicken heart (optional)
¼ pound fresh mushrooms, thinly sliced
1 small garlic clove, minced (optional)
3 tablespoons all-purpose flour
2 cups canned chicken broth, or turkey or chicken stock
¼ cup dry white wine
¼ cup heavy cream
¼ teaspoon rubbed sage
Salt and pepper

1. If desired, partially freeze the turkey breast, to firm slightly for easier slicing. Thinly slice the turkey across the grain, about ¼ inch thick.

2. Melt 1 tablespoon of the butter in a large heavy skillet over moderate heat. Add the chicken liver and heart and sauté just until cooked through, 2 to 3 minutes. Remove and reserve. Add the mushrooms and sauté just until tender, adding 1 or 2 tablespoons of water if the pan seems dry. Remove and reserve. Add the remaining 1 tablespoon butter and sauté the garlic for 1 minute. Stir in the flour and cook for 30 seconds longer. Add the chicken broth, wine, cream and sage. Stirring constantly, bring to a boil. Simmer for 1 to 2 minutes. Add the turkey slices and cook just until done, 2 to 3 minutes. Finely chop the liver and heart and add, along with the sautéed mushrooms. Season with salt and pepper to taste. Serve hot.

Calories *278*   **Protein** *29 gm*   **Fat** *14 gm*   **Carbohydrate** *8 gm*   **Sodium** *644 mg*   **Cholesterol** *106 mg*

STIR-FRIED TURKEY WITH SNOW PEAS, MUSHROOMS AND WATER CHESTNUTS

This tasty version of Moo Goo Gai Pan is made with turkey breast. It is best prepared with fresh water chestnuts (instructions on page 150) but if they are unavailable, use canned.

MAKES 4 SERVINGS

SAUCE:
- *1 tablespoon cornstarch*
- *⅓ cup canned chicken broth or stock*
- *1 tablespoon reduced-sodium soy sauce*
- *1 tablespoon rice wine or dry sherry*
- *½ teaspoon sugar*
- *½ teaspoon Oriental sesame oil*

STIR-FRY:
- *1 tablespoon peanut oil or vegetable oil*
- *1 tablespoon minced fresh ginger*
- *1 medium garlic clove, minced or crushed through a press*
- *1 cup chopped Napa cabbage or other green cabbage*
- *1 medium (4-ounce) onion, slivered lengthwise*
- *½ pound fresh snow peas, ends trimmed (or substitute green beans cut in 1½-inch lengths)*
- *1 cup thinly sliced water chestnuts, halved (see instructions for dealing with fresh water chestnuts, page 150) or 1 can (8 oz.) water chestnuts*
- *½ pound fresh mushrooms, thinly sliced*

- *1 pound skinless boned turkey breast, cut across the grain into thin slices about 1 by 2 inches*
- *3 medium scallions, quartered lengthwise and cut into 2-inch lengths*

1. MAKE THE SAUCE: In a small bowl, dissolve the cornstarch in the chicken broth. Stir in the soy sauce, rice wine, sugar and sesame oil.

2. MAKE THE STIR-FRY: Heat a large heavy wok or Dutch oven over high heat. Add the peanut oil, ginger and garlic; stir-fry for 10 seconds. Add the cabbage and onion and stir-fry for 1 to 2 minutes to soften. At any time during stir-frying if the wok seems dry, add 1 or 2 tablespoons of water to encourage the cooking. Add the snow peas and water chestnuts and stir-fry for 1 minute. Add the mushrooms and stir-fry for 1 minute longer. Add the turkey and the scallions and stir-fry until just cooked through, 1 to 2 minutes. Stir the sauce and add; cook until thickened. Turn out onto a serving platter or individual plates and serve hot, right away.

Calories *268*   **Protein** *31 gm*   **Fat** *6 gm*   **Carbohydrate** *21 gm*   **Sodium** *321 mg*   **Cholesterol** *70 mg*

MEAT LOAF WITH BROWNED VEGETABLES

When a quantity of chopped well-browned vegetables is added to beef, a bigger, moister, tastier, less-fattening meat loaf is created. This is good hot with Mashed Potatoes and Low Calorie Gravy (page 112) or cold with Old-Fashioned Potato Salad (page 43).

MAKES 6 SERVINGS

*1 tablespoon olive oil or other
 vegetable oil*
*1½ cups finely chopped cabbage
 (6 ounces)*
1 cup finely diced celery
1 medium (4-ounce) onion, chopped
*1 small garlic clove, minced or crushed
 through a press*
*1 pound extra-lean ground beef, such
 as round or sirloin*
2 large eggs
½ cup plain dry bread crumbs
1 can (8-ounce) tomato sauce
¼ cup chopped parsley
½ teaspoon dried basil, crumbled
½ teaspoon celery salt
¼ teaspoon salt
⅛ teaspoon black pepper

1. Preheat the oven to 325°. Spray a 9-by-5-by-3-inch loaf pan with nonstick vegetable spray, or lightly oil. Line crosswise with a sheet of aluminum foil (the ends don't need lining) so it extends an inch upward along the two long sides. Lightly spray the foil.

2. Spoon the olive oil into a large non-reactive skillet and place over moderate heat. Add the cabbage, celery, onion and garlic; sauté, stirring frequently and adding 1 to 2 tablespoons water each time the vegetables seem dry (4 to 6 tablespoons will be needed), until lightly browned and softened, 10 to 15 minutes. Turn out and let cool almost to room temperature.

3. Crumble the beef into a large bowl. Add the eggs, bread crumbs, ½ cup of the tomato sauce, the parsley, basil, celery salt, salt, pepper and the sautéed vegetables. Mix with your hands or a big spoon until evenly blended. Turn into the prepared pan. Smooth to level the top. Spread the remaining ½ cup tomato sauce over the top. Bake in the center of the oven for 1 hour, just until cooked through. Let stand for 10 to 15 minutes. Pull out of the pan by lifting the aluminum foil; discard the foil. Cut into 12 slices. Serve 2 slices per person, hot or cold (if serving cold, slice when chilled).

Calories 287   *Protein* 18 gm   *Fat* 18 gm   *Carbohydrate* 13 gm   *Sodium* 596 mg   *Cholesterol* 144 mg

RED AND YELLOW STUFFED PEPPERS *Roasting and peeling the sweet peppers before stuffing them gives them a wonderful light smoky flavor. These peppers are sprinkled with coarse yellow cornmeal and sautéed to make an attractive presentation. They are especially good with the Spanish Rice Timbales on page 121.*

MAKES 4 SERVINGS

2 large (8-ounce) red bell peppers
2 large (8-ounce) yellow bell peppers
½ pound extra-lean ground beef
1 cup fresh, frozen or canned corn kernels
1 medium (4-ounce) onion, grated
1 medium garlic clove, minced or crushed through a press
⅓ cup chopped cilantro (fresh coriander)
2 tablespoons fresh lime juice
1 teaspoon dried oregano, crumbled
1 teaspoon ground cumin
¼ teaspoon ground cinnamon
1 teaspoon salt
¼ teaspoon black pepper
2 teaspoons coarse yellow cornmeal
1½ teaspoons vegetable oil
1 cup canned chicken broth or stock

1. Roast the peppers directly over a gas flame or under the broiler as close to the heat as possible, turning until charred all over. Place in a plastic bag, twisting the top to enclose them, and let steam in the refrigerator for about 5 minutes. Working over a colander, peel the peppers by rubbing the skins away lightly under gently running water. Cut the peppers in half lengthwise, remove the seeds, ribs and stems; drain.

2. In a medium bowl, stir together the ground beef, corn, onion, garlic, cilantro, lime juice, oregano, cumin, cinnamon, salt and pepper. Place one pepper half peeled side down, on a flat surface and add about ¼ cup of the filling. Fold the pepper over, taco-style, to cover the filling. Repeat with the remaining pepper halves and filling.

3. Sprinkle ¼ teaspoon of the cornmeal over each stuffed pepper half. Coat a large heavy skillet (one that will hold all the peppers in a single layer) with the vegetable oil and heat over moderately high heat. Add all of the peppers, cornmeal-coated sides down, and brown well, 2 to 3 minutes. Turn; add the chicken broth to the skillet and bring to a boil over moderate heat. Cover and reduce the heat to low; simmer until cooked through, 15 to 20 minutes. Transfer the stuffed peppers to a warm platter. Boil the broth until reduced to about ¼ cup. Drizzle the broth over the peppers. Serve hot with Spanish Rice Timbales, if desired.

***Calories** 236   **Protein** 14 gm   **Fat** 13 gm   **Carbohydrate** 18 gm   **Sodium** 849 mg   **Cholesterol** 39 mg*

BEEF WITH SPICY SPINACH SAUCE *This streamlined version of the classic East Indian meat stew contains twice as much spinach and half the meat it normally would. Less than a quarter of the oil usually required for browning the ingredients is called for here and the cooking techniques have been adjusted. Serve with the Fragrant Basmati Rice Timbales (page 119) or with the fresh peach or mango chutney (pages 153 and 152).*

MAKES 8 SERVINGS

2 tablespoons vegetable oil
2 pounds lean trimmed beef chuck, sirloin or round, cut into ³/₄-inch cubes
4 medium (4-ounce) onions, chopped
3 medium garlic cloves, minced
¹/₄ cup finely chopped fresh ginger
2 tablespoons curry powder
1 tablespoon ground cumin
1 tablespoon ground coriander
¹/₂ teaspoon freshly grated nutmeg
¹/₄ teaspoon cayenne pepper
3 tablespoons all-purpose flour
1 can (8-ounce) tomato sauce
¹/₂ cup plain lowfat yogurt, at room temperature
10 whole cardamom pods, cracked
5 whole cloves
1 bay leaf
1 (3-inch) cinnamon stick
2 teaspoons salt
4 pounds fresh spinach

1. Spoon 2 teaspoons of the vegetable oil into a large heavy nonstick Dutch oven or saucepan over moderately high heat. Add half of the beef, stir once to distribute in an even layer and cook without stirring, for about 3 minutes, until deep golden brown. Stir once again and brown for 2 to 3 minutes longer. Transfer to a bowl and repeat with 2 teaspoons more oil and the rest of the beef. Set aside.

2. Spoon the remaining 2 teaspoons oil into the pan and add the onions. Working over high to moderately-high heat (you'll have to adjust it as you work), brown-fry the onions. This classic Indian technique requires at least 15 minutes of continuous stirring, until they are deep caramel-brown in color. Each time the onions begin to stick or seem dry, add 1 or 2 tablespoons of water and continue stirring and browning. You will need 8 to 12 tablespoons of water in all. As the onions brown more, be sure to regulate the heat and stir constantly.

3. Add the garlic and ginger and stir-fry for 1 minute. Add the curry powder, cumin, coriander, nutmeg, cayenne and flour; stir for 1 minute. The mixture will be very dry. Add the tomato sauce and stir to make a paste. Cook for 1 to 2 minutes, until thick. Stir in the yogurt.

164

Add the cardamom pods, cloves, bay leaf, cinnamon stick and salt. Return the meat to the pan and add 3 cups of water. Bring to a boil, stirring frequently, over moderate heat. Cover, lower the heat and simmer, stirring once in a while, until the meat is very tender, about 2 hours. **(This recipe can be prepared to this point 1 to 3 days ahead.)**

4. If you have prepared the beef ahead, reheat it before adding the spinach. Wash the spinach in a large sinkful of cool water and pull off and discard any coarse stems. Put all of the spinach in a large heavy pot (such as a Dutch oven), packing it in. Cover and place over moderately high heat and cook, turning the mass of leaves over once or twice, just until wilted down and cooked. Drain in a colander, pressing out the spinach juice (which should be reserved for another use). Coarsely chop the spinach. You should have about 4 cups. Add it to the beef and heat for 2 to 3 minutes. Serve hot.

Calories 319   *Protein* 29 gm   *Fat* 16 gm   *Carbohydrate* 18 gm   *Sodium* 815 mg   *Cholesterol* 75 mg

---

S TUFFED EGGPLANT *This is one of my favorite recipes with its filling of corn and beans and ground beef that tastes all American to me. Just ½ pound of lean ground beef and a single tablespoon of olive oil are incorporated into this dish which feeds four people quite substantially. Serve with a mixed salad.*

MAKES 4 SERVINGS

2 medium (1 pound) firm eggplants
2 teaspoons olive oil
1 medium (4-ounce) onion, chopped
2 large garlic cloves, minced or crushed through a press
1 cup (4 ounces) green beans cut in ½-inch lengths
¾ cup raw corn kernels, cut from 2 to 3 medium ears, or use frozen or canned
1 can (28-ounce) whole tomatoes, in their juice

1 teaspoon dried basil, crumbled
1 teaspoon dried oregano, crumbled
1 teaspoon ground cumin
¼ teaspoon black pepper
½ pound very lean ground beef
2 tablespoons all-purpose flour
Salt
¼ cup shredded Swiss cheese or Cheddar cheese (1 ounce)

1. Preheat the oven to 375°. Halve the eggplants lengthwise. With a paring knife, cut around the inside of each

eggplant half leaving a ½-inch shell. With a spoon, scoop out the eggplant flesh. Chop the flesh into ½-inch pieces. Put the shells in a 13-by-9-inch baking pan.

2. Spoon the olive oil into a nonreactive large skillet and place over moderate heat. Add the onion and sauté to soften, 3 to 5 minutes. Add the garlic and cook for 30 seconds longer. Add the green beans and corn; sauté for about 2 minutes, adding 1 or 2 tablespoons water if the vegetables begin to stick or seem dry. Stir in the eggplant and cook to soften over moderately high heat, 3 to 4 minutes, adding 2 to 3 tablespoons water if the mixture seems dry.

3. Place a strainer over a bowl and drain the tomatoes, cutting them in half to drain further. Coarsely chop the tomatoes. Reserve ½ cup of the tomato juice.

Add the chopped tomatoes to the eggplant mixture along with the basil, oregano, cumin and pepper and cook over moderately high heat to evaporate most of the liquid, 3 to 4 minutes. Remove from the heat.

4. Crumble the ground beef in a medium skillet and brown well over moderately high heat. Stir in the flour and cook for 1 minute. Add the beef to the eggplant mixture and cook for about 2 minutes over moderate heat. Stir in salt to taste. Spoon into the four eggplant halves, spreading the filling completely over the top edges of each shell. Spoon 2 tablespoons of the reserved tomato juice over the top of each; top each with 1 tablespoon of the Swiss cheese. Bake for 45 to 55 minutes, until tender and the tops are browned. Let stand for 10 minutes. Serve hot.

Calories 343 **Protein** 19 gm **Fat** 15 gm **Carbohydrate** 37 gm **Sodium** 397 mg **Cholesterol** 46 mg

VEAL- AND PORK-STUFFED CABBAGE ROLLS

Besides being innovative and very low in calories, these zesty cabbage rolls, with their creamy sauce, are high in fiber and they reheat very well. Each serving makes a large, hearty dinner.

MAKES 6 SERVINGS

1 large (3-pound) head of green cabbage, cored
⅓ cup brown rice
½ pound very lean ground veal
½ pound very lean ground pork
1 egg
¼ cup minced fresh dill plus 3 sprigs of fresh dill
1 teaspoon grated lemon zest
1 teaspoon salt
¼ teaspoon black pepper
1 medium (4-ounce) onion, grated
3 tablespoons fresh lemon juice
1 large garlic clove, minced or crushed through a press
¼ cup tomato paste
2 cups canned chicken broth or stock
1 lemon, cut into thin slices
2 tablespoons all-purpose flour
¼ cup cream cheese (2 ounces)
Salt
Sprigs of dill and lemon wedges, for garnish

1. Pour about 2 inches of water into a large stovetop casserole or Dutch oven and bring to a boil over high heat. Place the cabbage in the water and partially cover the pan. Cook, turning occasionally, until the outer leaves are tender and translucent, about 10 minutes. Remove the outer translucent leaves and return the cabbage to the water. Cook until more leaves are tender, 3 to 5 minutes. Repeat as necessary until all of the cabbage is cooked.

2. Pour about 6 cups of water into a medium saucepan and bring to a boil over high heat. Slowly add the rice so that the water continues to boil. Cook, stirring occasionally, until just tender, about 20 minutes. Drain the rice in a sieve and transfer it to a large bowl.

3. Add the veal, pork, egg, 3 tablespoons of the minced dill, the lemon zest, salt, pepper, onion, lemon juice, garlic and tomato paste to the rice; stir to blend well.

4. Choose the 12 best cabbage leaves and set them aside. Finely chop all of the remaining cabbage. Stir 1 cup of the chopped cabbage into the rice filling; arrange the rest in a large shallow glass baking pan (13-by-9-by-2 inch is perfect).

5. Preheat the oven to 375°. Using a paring knife, devein the 12 remaining cabbage leaves by slicing off the raised portion of the veins flush to the leaves. Place one leaf, deveined-side down, on a flat surface. Place about ⅓ cup of the filling on the lower third of the leaf and pat it into a 4-inch log. Fold the bottom (stem end) of the leaf upward over 1½ inches of the filling. Fold the two sides inward and roll up tightly to enclose the filling. Place seam-side down in a single layer over the bed of chopped cabbage. Repeat with the remaining cabbage leaves and filling to make three crosswise rows of cabbage rolls. Pour the chicken broth over the stuffed cabbage and top with the lemon slices and the 3 sprigs of dill. Cover tightly with a double layer of aluminum foil. Bake for 1 hour. Let stand, covered, at room temperature for 1 hour.

6. Uncover the casserole and discard the lemon slices and dill sprigs. With a slotted spoon transfer the cabbage rolls to a hot platter. Pour the juices and chopped cabbage into a medium nonreactive saucepan. Gradually sift in the flour, whisking until smoothly blended. Add the cream cheese and cook over moderate heat, stirring, until melted. Bring to a boil, stirring constantly, and cook until thickened, 2 to 3 minutes. Stir in the remaining 1 tablespoon minced dill. Season the sauce with salt to taste.

7. To serve, allow 2 stuffed cabbage rolls and 1/2 cup sauce per person. (I like to cut each roll into 5 pieces and slightly overlap them on each plate.) Garnish each plate with a sprig of dill and a lemon wedge.

Calories 298   *Protein* 21 gm   *Fat* 13 gm   *Carbohydrate* 27 gm   *Sodium* 915 mg   *Cholesterol* 109 mg

STUFFED POLENTA WITH MEAT SAUCE *Rich, filling and satisfying, this layered cornmeal concoction is Italian comfort food for people who like to eat. Polenta is a cornmeal staple in much of Italy. You will need two 8- or 9-inch square pans.*

MAKES 4 SERVINGS

½ teaspoon salt
¾ cup coarse yellow cornmeal
½ pound extra-lean ground beef
1 medium (4-ounce) onion, chopped
1 large garlic clove, minced or crushed
  through a press
1 teaspoon dried basil, crumbled
½ teaspoon dried oregano, crumbled
¼ teaspoon dried rosemary, crumbled
¼ teaspoon black pepper
2 tablespoons tomato paste
1 can (16-ounce) peeled Italian
  tomatoes, with their juice
2 tablespoons dry white or red wine
½ cup part-skim mozzarella (2 ounces),
  cut into ½-inch dice
⅓ cup freshly grated Parmesan cheese
  (1⅓ ounces)

1. To prepare the polenta, pour 1½ cups of water into a heavy medium saucepan, add ¼ teaspoon of the salt and bring to a boil over high heat. Place the cornmeal in a small bowl and stir in ¾ cup cold water to moisten it. Stir the cornmeal mixture and add it all at once to the boiling water, stirring constantly. Reduce the heat to low and simmer, stirring constantly, until very thick, about 10 minutes. Lightly coat two 8- or 9-inch square baking pans with nonstick vegetable cooking spray (or lightly oil). Working quickly, spread half of the polenta into each pan, smoothing it out until level (if necessary, dip your fingers in cold water and pat the surface until it is level). Let cool in the refrigerator to firm up.

2. Adjust a shelf to the upper third of the oven and preheat to 450°.

3. To make the sauce, crumble the ground beef into a heavy medium saucepan; lightly brown over moderate heat until half-cooked. Add the onion and garlic and sauté until the onion is softened, about 3 minutes. Drain off the fat. Stir in the basil, oregano, rosemary, pepper and tomato paste. Add the tomatoes and their juice, breaking up the tomatoes with a spoon. Bring to a boil over moderate heat. Reduce the heat and simmer, stirring frequently, until thick and rich, about 15 minutes. Stir in the re-

maining ¼ teaspoon salt and the wine. Remove from the heat.

4. When the polenta has set, spread half of the tomato-meat sauce evenly over the polenta in one of the pans. Top with half of the mozzarella and half of the Parmesan. Invert the other layer of polenta over the filling and tap the pan so it un-

molds on top. Spread with the remaining tomato meat sauce and sprinkle with the remaining mozzarella and Parmesan cheeses. Bake until hot, bubbly and lightly browned, 15 to 20 minutes. Let stand for 10 minutes. Cut into 4 equal squares and serve hot.

Calories 339   *Protein* 22 gm   *Fat* 12 gm   *Carbohydrate* 35 gm   *Sodium* 772 mg   *Cholesterol* 49 mg

---

MY SKINNY CHEESEBURGERS *I don't like big fat burgers. There's too much meat for the bread. Instead, I shape just a quarter cup of extra-lean ground beef into very thin rounds and serve them on buns with cheese and grilled onions. You can replace the mayonnaise and ketchup with the Thousand Island Dressing on page 56 and lower calories and sodium even further. If the mood strikes, serve them with the Broiled French Fries (page 114).*

MAKES 4 SERVINGS

4 hamburger buns (4 inches in diameter)
1 cup extra-lean ground beef such as round or sirloin (about 9 ounces)
½ teaspoon vegetable oil
4 medium-size onion slices (¼-inch thick)
½ cup shredded sharp Cheddar cheese (2 ounces)
4 teaspoons ketchup
4 teaspoons mayonnaise
8 small thin dill pickle slices

1. Preheat a broiler or toaster oven for toasting the buns and melting the cheese. Toast the buns.

2. Place four 6-inch squares of waxed paper on a flat surface. Scoop ¼ cup of the ground beef onto each and pat into 4 very thin 4-inch patties. Leave the patties on the paper and use your fingertip to poke a small hole in the center of each one to minimize shrinkage during cooking.

3. Place a large nonstick or well-seasoned skillet over moderately high heat.

Lightly coat with the oil. Plop in the burgers, aiming for the right spot because you won't be able to reposition them once they hit the skillet. Peel off and discard the waxed paper. Drop in the onion slices around the burgers and cook for about 2 minutes, until the burgers are browned. Turn with a spatula and cook 1 minute longer, or to taste. The onion slices will take a little longer than the burgers; cook just to soften, 3 to 5 minutes.

4. Place each burger on the bottom half of a toasted bun. Sprinkle each with 2 tablespoons of the cheese. Run under the broiler just until melted, about 1 minute. Spread the bun tops with 1 teaspoon ketchup and 1 teaspoon mayonnaise. Add the sautéed onions and 2 dill pickle slices to each, place over the burgers and serve hot.

Calories *346*   **Protein** *19 gm*   **Fat** *19 gm*   **Carbohydrate** *24 gm*   **Sodium** *517 mg*   **Cholesterol** *60 mg*

FLASH-FRIED LAMB WITH ASPARAGUS AND SCALLIONS *Here is the ultimate Chinese springtime stir-fry to take advantage of the fresh asparagus and tender young lamb in the market at that time of year. It is made with just a fraction of the oil that most stir-fries contain.*

MAKES 4 SERVINGS

¾ pound lean boneless leg of lamb, cut in thin slices across the grain and then into 1-inch pieces
2 tablespoons plus 2 teaspoons soy sauce
2 tablespoons dry sherry
½ teaspoon black pepper
1 tablespoon rice vinegar
2 teaspoons cornstarch
½ teaspoon Oriental sesame oil
2 tablespoons peanut or other vegetable oil
1 pound fresh medium asparagus, tough ends snapped off, cut on a severe diagonal into ½-inch lengths (12 ounces trimmed weight)
12 large scallions, (8 ounces), the entire stem cut in 2-inch lengths after trimming off an inch of the green top
1 garlic clove, minced or crushed through a press

1. In a medium bowl, stir together the lamb with 2 tablespoons of the soy sauce, the sherry and pepper. Let marinate at room temperature for 15 to 30 minutes.
2. In a small bowl, stir together the remaining 2 teaspoons soy sauce, the rice vinegar, cornstarch and sesame oil.

3. Place a large heavy wok over moderate heat. When very hot, pour in 1 tablespoon of the peanut oil and increase the heat to high. Add the lamb (most of the marinade will have been absorbed so just dump the whole thing in) and stir-fry for about 1 minute, until no longer red but not completely cooked. Remove and transfer to a plate.

4. Wipe out the wok with a paper towel and add the remaining 1 tablespoon peanut oil. Heat once again over high heat. Add the asparagus and stir-fry until barely tender, 1 to 2 minutes. Add the scallions and garlic and stir-fry for 1 minute, adding 1 to 2 tablespoons water to encourage the cooking and prevent sticking. Return the lamb and heat for a few seconds. Give the sauce mixture a good stir and add it all at once. Bring to a boil, stirring. If the sauce is too thick, add 1 to 2 tablespoons water. Serve hot.

Calories 220   *Protein* 20 gm   *Fat* 12 gm   *Carbohydrate* 8 gm   *Sodium* 750 mg   *Cholesterol* 60 mg

---

MOUSSAKA OF VEGETABLES AND LAMB *This tasty Greek casserole is made from layers of potato, eggplant, zucchini and a tomato-lamb filling and topped with a rich* Saltsa Aspri *(creamy white cheese sauce). It can be made hours ahead of time. If you can't find lean boneless lamb, try extra-lean ground lamb or beef instead. Classically, this is prepared with a huge amount of olive oil; here, the vegetables are broiled or boiled instead of fried. This is one of those casseroles that gains in flavor if served a day after it is made.*

MAKES 8 SERVINGS

VEGETABLES:
- *1 large (1½-pound) firm eggplant*
- *1 pound (3 medium) zucchini*
- *1 teaspoon olive oil*
- *1 pound (4 medium) red-skinned potatoes*

TOMATO-LAMB FILLING:
- *2 teaspoons olive oil*
- *1 large (8-ounce) onion, chopped*
- *2 large garlic cloves, minced or crushed through a press*
- *¾ pound lean trimmed boneless leg of lamb, thinly sliced across the grain and cut into 1-inch pieces*
- *1½ teaspoons dried oregano, crumbled*
- *½ teaspoon dried thyme, crumbled*
- *1 teaspoon salt*
- *¼ teaspoon black pepper*
- *1 can (35-ounce) whole tomatoes, with their juice, cut up*
- *½ cup plain dry bread crumbs*
- *1 large egg*

SALTSA ASPRI:
- *3 cups whole milk*
- *6 tablespoons all-purpose flour*
- *¼ teaspoon freshly grated nutmeg*
- *½ teaspoon salt*
- *¼ teaspoon black pepper*
- *½ cup freshly grated Parmesan cheese (2 ounces)*
- *1 large egg*

1. PREPARE THE VEGETABLES: Preheat the broiler. Using a fork or skewer, prick the eggplant all over, about 15 times. Place on a sheet of aluminum foil and broil until charred and soft, about 10 minutes. Turn and broil until soft inside and charred outside, about 5 minutes longer. Remove from the foil and transfer to a strainer to drain and cool. Leave the broiler on.

2. Wash and lightly brush the zucchini to remove any grit. Trim the ends away and cut the zucchini lengthwise into slices about ¼-inch thick. Line a broiler pan with aluminum foil. Arrange the zucchini in a single tight layer and broil for about 5 minutes to soften and evaporate some of the moisture content of the squash. Do not turn. Brush with the

1 teaspoon olive oil and return to the broiler. Broil until blistered and deep golden brown, 3 to 5 minutes longer. Remove, still on the foil, and let cool to room temperature.

3. Bring a medium pot of lightly salted water to a boil over high heat. Wash and scrub the potatoes. Cut them crosswise into slices about ¼-inch thick. Drop them into the boiling water and cook until just tender, 3 to 5 minutes after the water returns to the boil. Drain and reserve.

4. **MAKE THE TOMATO-LAMB FILLING:** Spoon the olive oil into a large nonreactive skillet and place over moderate heat. Add the onion and sauté until soft, 3 to 5 minutes (if the onion seems to need more oil to cook properly, add a tablespoon or 2 of water instead). Add the garlic and cook for 1 minute longer. Add the lamb and cook, stirring until it is no longer pink, 2 to 3 minutes. Stir in the oregano, thyme, salt, pepper and tomatoes with their juice. Bring to a boil, stirring frequently. Reduce the heat and simmer, stirring occasionally, until thick, 20 to 30 minutes. Remove from the heat and let cool slightly. With a fork, stir in ¼ cup of the bread crumbs and the egg.

5. Adjust an oven shelf to the top third of the oven and preheat to 375°. Lightly spray a 13-by-9-by-2-inch casserole or shallow baking dish with vegetable cooking spray. Sprinkle with the remaining ¼ cup bread crumbs.

6. Arrange all of the potatoes in a single or slightly overlapping layer over the bread crumbs. Spread with half of the tomato-lamb filling. Trim the stem end from the eggplant and cut the eggplant in half lengthwise. Scoop out the flesh in large pieces and coarsely chop it. Discard the skin. Arrange the chopped eggplant over the filling and top with the remaining filling. Spoon all of the zucchini over the top.

7. **MAKE THE SALTSA ASPRI:** Pour the milk into a heavy medium saucepan. Put the flour in a sieve held directly over the milk. Tap the sieve once lightly and whisk in the small amount of flour that sifts through. Repeat the tapping and whisking technique until all of the flour is gradually whisked in and the mixture is smooth. Add the nutmeg, salt and pepper. Place over moderate heat and, whisking constantly, bring to a boil. Reduce the heat and simmer, stirring, for 2 to 3 minutes, until thick. Remove from the heat. Stir in all but 2 tablespoons of the Parmesan cheese. In a large bowl, whisk the egg. Gradually whisk in the hot cheese sauce. Pour all of the sauce over the zucchini in the casserole. Sprinkle with the remaining 2 tablespoons Parmesan cheese. Bake in the top third of the oven until hot and golden brown on top, about 45 minutes. Let cool for at least 15 minutes. Cut into 8 large rectangles and serve hot; or cool, store in the refrigerator overnight and reheat in a 350° oven for 30 to 40 minutes before serving.

Calories 334 *Protein* 21 gm *Fat* 11 gm *Carbohydrate* 39 gm *Sodium* 875 mg *Cholesterol* 116 mg

---

CHAPTER SEVEN

DELECTABLE DESSERTS

When you crave something sweet, go ahead and indulge: These are desserts you can afford to enjoy. Here are sparkling versions of old favorites like the lemon-filled cake roll, berries with custard sauce or apple crisp with a toasted oat topping. For the occasion calling for drop-dead elegance, try the peach melba terrine with raspberry sauce or the tour de force chocolate souffle-filled crêpes with—yes!—chocolate sauce.

PEACH MELBA TERRINE WITH RASPBERRY SAUCE *Here is an elegant make-ahead dessert that can be prepared with fresh or frozen fruit. After unmolding, the terrine is sliced and served with cool raspberry sauce.*

MAKES 10 SERVINGS

TERRINE:

> ¼ cup brandy or Cognac
> 4 envelopes (¼ ounce each) unflavored gelatin
> 2 cups milk
> 2 large eggs, separated
> ½ cup sugar
> ½ cup white grape juice
> 3 tablespoons cornstarch
> 1 teaspoon vanilla extract
> ¼ teaspoon almond extract
> Pinch of salt
> 1½ cups diced, peeled—fresh or frozen peaches, thawed if frozen
> 1½ cups fresh or frozen raspberries, separated but not thawed

RASPBERRY SAUCE:

> 3 tablespoons sugar
> 1 teaspoon cornstarch
> ½ cup strained fresh orange juice
> 1 cup whole fresh or frozen raspberries, thawed if frozen
> 2 tablespoons brandy or Cognac

GARNISH:

> Whole raspberries and orange peel julienne

1. MAKE THE TERRINE: Lightly coat a 9-by-5-by-3-inch loaf pan with nonstick vegetable cooking spray (or lightly oil). Line with plastic wrap, smoothing out any bubbles with your fingertips. Lightly spray the plastic wrap (or very lightly oil).

2. Pour the brandy into a small bowl. Sprinkle the gelatin over it to moisten and then stir in ½ cup of the milk. Let the gelatin soften until needed.

3. Place the egg whites in a deep medium bowl and reserve. Place the egg yolks in a nonreactive medium saucepan. Stir ¼ cup of the sugar into the egg yolks along with the white grape juice, the remaining 1½ cups milk and the cornstarch. Whisk until the cornstarch dissolves and the egg yolks are blended. Bring to a boil over moderate heat, whisking constantly. Lower the heat and simmer, whisking, for 2 minutes. Remove from the heat and stir in the softened gelatin, vanilla and almond extract. Turn into a large bowl and let cool to room temperature, stirring occasionally. Do not leave the custard unattended at this stage, or the gelatin may set.

4. Add the pinch of salt to the egg whites and beat with an electric mixer at medium speed until foamy; gradually add the remaining sugar and beat, increasing the speed to high, until stiff, glossy peaks form. Do not overbeat.

5. Place the bowl of cooled custard over a bowl of crushed ice and, stirring constantly with a rubber spatula, cool just until it reaches a syrupy consistency. Spoon in about one-quarter of the beaten whites and quickly whisk together to lighten. Add the remaining whites and fold quickly together with a rubber spatula. Fold in the peaches and raspberries. Turn the mixture into the prepared pan. Cover and refrigerate for 8 hours or overnight, until set.

6. **MAKE THE RASPBERRY SAUCE:** In a nonreactive small saucepan, stir together the sugar and cornstarch. Stir in the orange juice and raspberries. Bring to a boil, whisking, over moderate heat. Lower the heat and simmer, stirring, for 1 minute. Remove from the heat and stir in the brandy. Strain through a fine sieve. Discard the raspberry seeds. Cover and chill until serving time.

7. Just before serving, invert a rectangular plate or serving tray over the terrine and unmold the terrine onto it. Peel off and discard the plastic. Cut the terrine into 10 slices, each about ¾-inch thick and place on dessert plates. Spoon about 1½ tablespoons of the raspberry sauce over each slice and garnish with whole raspberries and orange peel julienne.

| Calories 179 | Protein 6 gm | Fat 3 gm | Carbohydrate 28 gm | Sodium 54 mg | Cholesterol 62 mg |

APPLE CRISP WITH TOASTED OAT TOPPING

This quintessentially American dessert is reminiscent of apple pie but without the calorie-laden pastry. The crunchy oat topping remains crunchy, so the dessert can be made well ahead. A mere 4 tablespoons of sugar is used to serve 6 people.

MAKES 6 SERVINGS

½ cup old-fashioned rolled oats
1½ tablespoons butter, melted
¼ cup packed dark brown sugar
⅓ cup frozen unsweetened apple juice concentrate, thawed
⅛ teaspoon salt
2 pounds tart green cooking apples, such as Granny Smith or Greening (4 to 5 large)

1 tablespoon all-purpose flour
½ teaspoon ground cinnamon
¼ teaspoon freshly grated nutmeg

1. Adjust a shelf to the top third of the oven and preheat to 450°.
2. Coarsely chop the oats on a board. Place in a medium bowl and stir in the melted butter, brown sugar, 1 tablespoon of the apple juice and the salt.

3. Pare and core the apples (I pare them, quarter, then cut out cores from each portion); cut into ½-inch slices. Put the apple slices in a 12-by-8-inch shallow baking dish. Add the flour, cinnamon and nutmeg; toss to coat the apples. Pour in the remaining apple juice concentrate and toss again. Crumble the topping evenly over all. Bake until hot and bubbly, golden brown and crisp on the top, 20 to 25 minutes. Let stand for 10 minutes. Serve hot or warm. If you make it ahead of time and allow the dessert to cool completely, reheat it in a 325° oven for 15 minutes before serving.

Calories 190   *Protein* 2 gm   *Fat* 4 gm   *Carbohydrate* 40 gm   *Sodium* 82 mg   *Cholesterol* 8 mg

---

CHOCOLATE FLAN *You'd never guess you're eating a dessert low in calories when you indulge in one of these sinfully rich, cool and creamy Spanish flans.*

MAKES 4 SERVINGS

6 tablespoons sugar
¼ cup chocolate syrup
2 large whole eggs
1 large egg yolk
1 cup milk
½ cup evaporated milk
1½ teaspoons vanilla extract

1. Adjust a shelf to the bottom third of the oven and preheat to 325°. Lightly coat four 6-ounce custard cups (or fluted metal brioche tins) with nonstick vegetable cooking spray, or lightly oil.

2. In a small heavy saucepan, combine 5 tablespoons of the sugar with 3 tablespoons of water. Cook over moderate heat, stirring until the sugar dissolves. Increase the heat to moderately-high and cook until the syrup turns an amber color, 2 to 4 minutes. Working carefully and quickly, pour one-quarter of the caramel syrup into each prepared custard cup or mold and tilt the cups to coat on all surfaces. Let the caramel cool until needed.

3. In a medium bowl, whisk together the chocolate syrup, whole eggs and egg yolk until blended. In a small saucepan over moderate heat, combine the milk, evaporated milk and remaining 1 tablespoon sugar. Bring just to a simmer. Slowly whisk the hot milk into the egg mixture. Stir in the vanilla. Strain the mixture into a 4-cup measure. Pour into the prepared cups, dividing equally.

4. Place the cups in a shallow baking pan and pour in enough hot tap water to reach almost halfway up the sides of the cups. Cover loosely with a sheet of alu-

minum foil. Bake 35 to 40 minutes, until
a sharp knife inserted into the center
comes out clean. Remove the flans from
the hot water, let cool to room temperature. Refrigerate until well chilled, at
least 4 hours, or overnight, or as long as

a day or two.
5. To unmold, run a knife tip around
just the top edge of each flan and invert
them onto dessert plates. Pour any syrup
remaining in the molds over the flans.
Serve cold.

Calories 253   *Protein* 8 gm   *Fat* 9 gm   *Carbohydrate* 37 gm   *Sodium* 118 mg   *Cholesterol* 223 mg

---

CHOCOLATE SOUFFLÉ-STUFFED CRÊPES Light
and airy chocolate soufflé puffs like magic within delicately thin crêpes to add a perfect (and sensible) finishing touch to any elegant dinner party.

MAKES 6 SERVINGS

CRÊPES:
- ½ cup instant-blend flour (such as Wondra)
- ½ cup milk
- 1 large egg
- 2 teaspoons granulated sugar
- 1 teaspoon melted butter
- Pinch of salt

CHOCOLATE SAUCE:
- ¼ cup milk
- 2 ounces semisweet chocolate, finely chopped
- 1 teaspoon vanilla extract
- ½ teaspoon grated orange zest

CHOCOLATE SOUFFLÉ:
- ¼ cup milk
- 2 teaspoons instant-blend flour (such as Wondra)
- 2 ounces semisweet chocolate, finely chopped
- 2 large egg yolks, at room temperature
- 1 teaspoon vanilla extract
- Pinch of salt
- 3 large egg whites, at room temperature
- 1 tablespoon granulated sugar

ASSEMBLY:
- 1 tablespoon confectioners' sugar
- 2 medium-size navel oranges, peeled and sectioned (optional)

1. **PREPARE THE CRÊPES:** Combine the flour, milk, egg, sugar, butter and salt in a blender or food processor. Process for 20 or 30 seconds, until smooth. Pour into a measuring cup.
2. Place a 6-inch nonstick skillet or crêpe pan over moderately high heat. When hot, lightly spray with nonstick vegetable cooking spray, or very lightly oil. Pour in just enough of the batter (about 3 tablespoons) to coat the bottom of the pan. (The crêpes should be thin.) Cook for about 15 seconds, or until the edges are

firm and lightly browned. Turn with a spatula and cook for about 15 seconds longer. Transfer to a waxed paper-lined plate and top with a sheet of waxed paper. Repeat, stacking the crêpes on the plate with waxed paper in between. (**The crêpes can be prepared 1 to 2 days ahead, wrapped and refrigerated, or frozen for up to 3 months.**)

3. MAKE THE CHOCOLATE SAUCE: In a small saucepan over moderate heat, bring the milk just to a simmer. Remove the pan from the heat and add the chocolate, stirring until melted. Stir in the vanilla and orange zest. Reserve at room temperature.

4. MAKE THE CHOCOLATE SOUFFLÉ FILLING: Adjust a shelf to the center of the oven and preheat to 350°. Lightly coat a large baking sheet or jelly roll pan with nonstick vegetable cooking spray, or very lightly oil.

5. In a small heavy saucepan over moderate heat, whisk the milk and flour together until smooth. Bring the mixture to a boil, reduce the heat to low, and simmer, whisking constantly, until thickened. Remove from the heat and stir in the chocolate until smooth and melted. Whisk in the egg yolks, vanilla and salt. Scrape into a medium bowl.

6. Wash a medium bowl and egg beaters with scalding hot water to make sure that they are absolutely grease-free (or egg whites will not fluff up properly). Dry thoroughly. Add the egg whites to the bowl and beat with a hand-held electric mixer set at low speed until foamy. Gradually increase the speed to medium-high and continue beating the egg whites until they start to form soft peaks. Add the granulated sugar and continue beating just until the whites form stiff glossy peaks.

7. Using a rubber spatula, stir one-third of the egg whites into the chocolate mixture to lighten it. Fold in the remaining egg whites.

8. ASSEMBLY: Fold the crêpes in half and arrange, evenly spaced, on the prepared baking sheet. Open a crêpe and spoon about one-sixth of the soufflé filling onto the bottom half of the crêpe. Fold the top half of the crêpe over to cover the filling. Repeat the procedure with the remaining filling and crêpes. Sift the confectioners' sugar evenly over the tops.

9. Bake for 8 to 10 minutes, or until the filling is puffed. Immediately transfer to six warmed dessert plates. Spoon the chocolate sauce over the crêpes. Garnish the plates with the orange segments, if desired, and serve at once.

Calories 254 *Protein* 7 gm *Fat* 12 gm *Carbohydrate* 32 gm *Sodium* 114 mg *Cholesterol* 144 mg

---

GINGER-STUFFED BAKED APPLES *These beautiful ginger and cinnamon-scented baked apples make a lovely dessert. They are addictively delicious and have a soothing texture.*

MAKES 4 SERVINGS

½ lemon
4 large baking apples, such as Rome Beauty
½ cup chopped walnuts (2 ounces)
3 tablespoons sugar
1 tablespoon shredded fresh ginger
½ teaspoon powdered ginger
½ teaspoon ground cinnamon
1 egg yolk
2 tablespoons light or dark brown sugar
1 tablespoon butter, softened

1. Adjust a shelf to the top third of the oven and preheat to 375°.
2. Squeeze the lemon half; you will need 2 teaspoons of the juice. Cut the lemon half in two; reserve for rubbing the apples.
3. Cut off about ½ inch from the top of each apple and with a paring knife, pare off about ½ inch of skin from around the top of each apple. Rub the cut surfaces with lemon. With a paring knife and spoon, cut out the cores to make room for the stuffing. Rub all the cut surfaces with the lemon. Stand the apples upright in an 8-inch square baking pan.
4. In a food processor, combine ⅓ cup of the walnuts, the sugar, fresh ginger, powdered ginger, cinnamon and egg yolk. Process to finely grind the nuts. Spoon the filling into the center of each apple, dividing equally. In a small bowl, stir together the brown sugar and butter. Press it onto the cut surfaces of the apples. Sprinkle the tops with the reserved walnuts. Pour ½ cup water into the pan around the apples. Bake until tender, 45 minutes to 1 hour. Cool for at least 15 minutes before serving hot or warm.

Calories 318   *Protein 3 gm*   *Fat 14 gm*   *Carbohydrate 50 gm*   *Sodium 35 mg*   *Cholesterol 76 mg*

PEARS WITH BERRY-WINE GLAZE *This elegant dessert tastes even better when chilled for several hours. The flavor of zinfandel, the fruity red wine, is complemented by the raspberries and orange in this sophisticated version of the classic dish.*

MAKES 4 SERVINGS

1 large orange
2 cups zinfandel wine
½ cup sugar
5 whole cloves
1 cinnamon stick (3-inch)
4 medium-size Bosc pears, (6 ounces each), with stems intact
1 cup frozen unsweetened raspberries

1. Slice off 3 thin strips of peel from the orange (each about 1 by 3 inches). Cut the orange in half crosswise and squeeze out the juice (you should have about ½ cup). In a nonreactive medium saucepan (just large enough to hold the pears upright), combine the wine, sugar, cloves, cinnamon and reserved orange peel and juice. Bring to a boil over moderate heat. Reduce the heat to low and simmer while you prepare the pears.
2. Slice off just a sliver from the bottom of each pear (so that they will sit flat). With a swivel-blade peeler, peel the pears, working lengthwise. Stand them upright in the pan and increase the heat slightly. Poach the pears until tender when pierced with a toothpick, 3 to 5 minutes. Remove with a slotted spoon. Discard the orange peel. Add the raspberries to the wine mixture and boil over moderate heat for 5 minutes. Force through a sieve and discard the raspberry seeds, cloves and cinnamon stick. Return the purée to the pan and keep at a slow boil until reduced to ⅔ cup. Let cool to room temperature, about 10 minutes.
3. Stand the pears upright in a dish just large enough to hold them and spoon the glaze over the tops. Cover and chill thoroughly. Place 1 pear on each of 4 dessert plates and spoon the chilled glaze over them. Serve cold.

Calories *225*   **Protein** *1 gm*   **Fat** *1 gm*   **Carbohydrate** *57 gm*   **Sodium** *7 mg*   **Cholesterol** *0 mg*

ZESTY LEMON CAKE ROLL

This is one of those old-fashioned desserts that seem absolutely contemporary; and in this marvelous reworking, each portion weighs in at just 212 calories. The light and fluffy cake and the refreshingly tart lemon filling are very easy to make, and the finished dessert is lovely to look at.

MAKES 8 SERVINGS

CAKE:
  3/4 cup all-purpose flour
  1 teaspoon baking powder
  4 large whole eggs
  Pinch of salt
  1/3 cup granulated sugar
  1 tablespoon confectioners' sugar

FILLING:
  2 medium lemons
  1/2 cup granulated sugar
  3 tablespoons cornstarch
  2 large egg yolks
  1 tablespoon butter
  1/2 teaspoon vanilla extract
  1 to 2 drops yellow food coloring
    (optional)
  1 tablespoon confectioners' sugar

1. **MAKE THE CAKE:** Position a shelf to the center of the oven and preheat to 375°. Lightly spray a 15-by-10-by-1-inch jelly-roll pan with nonstick vegetable cooking spray (or lightly oil). Line the pan with a sheet of parchment or waxed paper. Lightly spray or oil the paper. Lightly coat with flour, tapping out the excess. On a sheet of waxed paper or in a bowl, sift together the flour and baking powder.

2. Combine the eggs and salt in a large mixing bowl; beat with a hand-held electric mixer until foamy, about 1 minute. Continue beating as you gradually add the granulated sugar. Beat until thick and light, about 3 minutes. Sift half of the dry ingredients over the egg mixture and fold together with a rubber spatula. Sift the remaining dry ingredients over the top and quickly fold together, just until evenly blended. Quickly spread in an even layer in the prepared pan. Bake in the center of the oven until the center springs back when lightly touched and the edges of the cake begin to pull away from the sides of the pan, about 10 minutes. Remove from the oven and let cool for 1 minute. Sift the confectioners' sugar onto a clean kitchen towel and invert the cake onto it. Peel off the paper (if it should be stubborn, moisten slightly with a damp paper towel). With a serrated knife, trim about 1/4-inch of cake from each of the four sides. While still hot, starting at one short end, roll up the cake. Cover with the towel and let cool to room temperature.

3. **MAKE THE FILLING:** Using the fine side of a grater or a lemon zester, remove 1/2 teaspoon of zest from the lemons. Halve the lemons and squeeze to yield 1/4 cup fresh lemon juice.

4. In a nonreactive medium saucepan, stir together the granulated sugar and cornstarch. In a medium bowl, whisk to-

gether the egg yolks, ¼ cup fresh lemon juice and 1 cup of cold water. Whisk the mixture into the sugar mixture until smooth. Place over moderate heat and, stirring constantly, bring to a boil. Reduce the heat and simmer, stirring, for 2 minutes, until thick. Remove from the heat and stir in the butter, vanilla and food coloring. Turn into a shallow bowl and cover with waxed paper or plastic wrap placed directly on the surface. Let cool to room temperature.

5. ASSEMBLY: Unroll the cooled cake and spread all of the filling over it, leaving a ¼-inch border all around. Carefully reroll to enclose the filling and place, seam-side down, on a serving plate or board. Cover and refrigerate until set, about 2 hours. Sift the remaining 1 tablespoon confectioners' sugar over the top. Cut into 8 slices. (Although this cake can be served chilled, it will taste best if you allow it to come to room temperature for 30 minutes to an hour before slicing.)

Calories 212 **Protein** 5 gm **Fat** 6 gm **Carbohydrate** 35 gm **Sodium** 122 mg **Cholesterol** 209 mg

---

STRAWBERRY-CHAMPAGNE ZABAGLIONE
Champagne makes perfectly delicious zabaglione, and strawberries make this elegant last-minute dessert extra special.

MAKES 4 SERVINGS

*1 pint ripe strawberries, quickly rinsed
    and hulled
¼ cup sugar
2 large egg yolks
Pinch of salt
Pinch of cinnamon (optional)
⅓ cup brut Champagne*

1. Quarter the strawberries lengthwise and put them in a medium bowl with 2 tablespoons of the sugar. Stir to dissolve the sugar, mashing a few of the berries lightly for extra juiciness. (You can prepare the strawberries 1 hour ahead.)

2. Place 1 inch of water in the bottom of a double boiler over moderate heat. Reduce the heat to low and keep the water at a simmer.

3. In a medium bowl, stir together the remaining 2 tablespoons sugar, the egg yolks, salt and cinnamon. Beat with a hand-held electric mixer until light and fluffy, 2 to 3 minutes. With a rubber spatula, scrape the mixture into the top of the double boiler. Beat in about one-third of the Champagne. As soon as the mixture becomes foamy, beat in one-third more. Beat in the remaining Champagne and then beat over the simmering water until very fluffy, 8 to 10 minutes.

4. Place about 2 tablespoons of the strawberries in each of 4 stemmed glasses or dessert dishes. Spoon in one-fourth of the zabaglione and top with the remaining strawberries. Serve immediately.

Calories 104   *Protein* 2 gm   *Fat* 3 gm   *Carbohydrate* 18 gm   *Sodium* 39 mg   *Cholesterol* 136 mg

---

FRESH BERRIES WITH OLD-FASHIONED CUSTARD SAUCE *If you don't want to serve eight at one sitting, keep the custard sauce in the refrigerator and serve ¼ cup of it with each ½ cup of fresh berries. My grandmother used to make this, but she used a little more sugar than I do.*

MAKES 8 SERVINGS

2 large eggs
⅓ cup sugar
1 tablespoon cornstarch
1¾ cups milk
½ teaspoon grated orange or lemon zest (optional)
1 teaspoon vanilla extract
1 to 2 drops almond extract
1 pint fresh strawberries, hulled
½ pint fresh raspberries
½ pint fresh blackberries or blueberries

1. In the top of a double boiler (off the heat), whisk the eggs until blended.
2. On a sheet of waxed paper, stir together the sugar and cornstarch; add to the eggs and whisk until smooth. Gradually whisk in the milk. Add the orange zest and place over boiling water. Stirring constantly, cook until thick enough to coat a spoon (175°), 12 to 15 minutes. Immediately place the pan in a larger pan of cold water to stop the cooking. Stir for a minute or so. Pour into a bowl and stir in the vanilla and almond extracts. Cover with a sheet of plastic wrap placed directly on the surface and let cool to room temperature. Refrigerate until well chilled.
3. Meanwhile, prepare the berries. Rinse the strawberries very quickly. Drain and place on paper towels to dry. Do not rinse the raspberries and black berries unless they are very dirty. Then, do so quickly and drain quickly on paper towels. Put ½ cup of the berries into each of 8 dessert dishes. Top each with ¼ cup of the cold custard sauce. Serve cold.

Calories 119   *Protein* 4 gm   *Fat* 4 gm   *Carbohydrate* 19 gm   *Sodium* 44 mg   *Cholesterol* 76 mg

---

HONEYDEW MELON WITH STRAWBERRY SAUCE *Here is a refreshingly light and satisfying dessert. I love its cool green color set off by the crimson strawberry sauce.*

MAKES 4 SERVINGS

2 cups sliced fresh strawberries (see NOTE)
2 tablespoons sugar
1 teaspoon vanilla extract
4 wedges (3-inch) ripe honeydew melon

NOTE: Quickly rinse the berries in cool water and remove the hulls before slicing.

1. In a food processor or blender, combine the strawberries, sugar and vanilla; purée. If making ahead of time, cover and refrigerate.

2. Cut each wedge of honeydew melon into thirds to make three 1-inch wedges. Run a knife blade between the rind and the flesh to separate. Discard the rinds. Arrange 3 wedges on each dessert plate and spoon about ¼ cup of the strawberry sauce over each.

Calories 118   *Protein* 1 gm   *Fat* .5 gm   *Carbohydrate* 30 gm   *Sodium* 20 mg   *Cholesterol* 0 mg

CHOCOLATE-COFFEE ICE *Powerfully seductive, this simple Italian-style ice is a welcome treat after dinner or brunch.*

MAKES 8 SERVINGS

1 cup sugar
2 tablespoons unsweetened cocoa powder
4 cups hot, strong (French or Italian roast) brewed coffee
2 teaspoons vanilla extract
Grated zest of 1 small lemon
1 large egg white

1. In a large bowl, sift together the sugar and cocoa. Gradually whisk in the hot coffee until the sugar and cocoa dissolve. Set the bowl over a bowl of ice and stir for about 10 minutes (or let cool to room temperature and then chill briefly). Stir in the vanilla and lemon zest.

2. Pour the coffee mixture into the container of an ice cream maker and freeze for half the time specified in the manufacturer's directions. In a small deep bowl, using a hand-held electric mixer, beat the egg white until foamy. Pour the white into the coffee mixture and continue freezing until the ice is hard. Remove from the freezer shortly before serving. Spoon into stemmed glasses.

Calories 109   *Protein* 1 gm   *Fat* .3 gm   *Carbohydrate* 27 gm   *Sodium* 10 mg   *Cholesterol* 0 mg

INDEX

Better Homes and Gardens®

The Idea Magazine
for Better Homes
and Families

For information on how you can have
Better Homes and Gardens delivered to your
door, write to: Mr. Robert Austin, P.O.
Box 4536, Des Moines, IA 50336.

ABOUT THE AUTHOR

Jim Fobel was born in Geneva, Ohio on the shores of Lake Erie, where he spent his early childhood before moving with his family to California. He took a degree in fine arts at the Otis Art Institute in Los Angeles, and on coming to New York City embarked on a career in professional cooking that now spans 20 years.

Mr. Fobel was for a number of years the director of the test kitchen for *Food & Wine* magazine and Food Editor for *Decorating & Craft Ideas*, as well as co-owner of the Picture Pie Boutique at Bloomingdale's. He has developed special low-calorie recipes for *Weight Watcher's Magazine* and *Cooking Light*, and is a frequent contributor to *Food & Wine*, *Bon Appetit* and *Family Circle* (where he is also food consultant). He is the author of **Beautiful Food** and of **Jim Fobel's Old-Fashioned Baking Book**, published in 1987 and winner of an IACP-Seagram's award and of a James Beard Foundation citation as one of the year's best cookbooks. Mr. Fobel lives in New York City.